Bookkeeping and Auditing: A Career Guide

Bookkeeping and Auditing: A Career Guide

Harry Watts

MURPHY & MOORE
www.murphy-moorepublishing.com

Bookkeeping and Auditing: A Career Guide
Harry Watts
ISBN: 978-1-63987-810-9 (Hardback)

MURPHY & MOORE
Murphy & Moore Publishing
1 Rockefeller Plaza,
New York City,
NY 10020, USA

Cataloging-in-Publication Data

Bookkeeping and auditing : a career guide / Harry Watts.
p. cm.
Includes bibliographical references and index.
ISBN 978-1-63987-810-9
1. Bookkeeping--Vocational guidance. 2. Auditing--Vocational guidance. 3. Accounting--Vocational guidance.
I. Watts, Harry.
HF5636 .B66 2023
657--dc23

Table of Contents

	Preface	**VII**
Chapter 1	**An Introduction to Bookkeeping and Auditing**	**1**
	• Bookkeeping	1
	• Auditing	3
	• Reasons to Consider a Career in Bookkeeping and Auditing	6
Chapter 2	**Skills for Becoming a Bookkeeper**	**9**
	• Bookkeeper	9
	• How to be a Bookkeeper	10
	• How to Bookkeep	11
	• How to do Bookkeeping for a Small Business	16
	• How to Become a Freelance Bookkeeper	24
	• How to Start a Freelance Bookkeeping and Payroll Service	25
	• How to Obtain a Bookkeeping Certificate Online	26
	• How to Study for a Bookkeeping Exam	29
Chapter 3	**Bookkeeping Processes**	**35**
	• How to Write an Accounting Ledger	35
	• How to Reconcile a General Ledger Account	46
	• How to Understand Debits and Credits	52
	• How to Understand and Set up a General Ledger	55
	• Double-entry Bookkeeping	60
	• How to do Double Entry Bookkeeping	62
	• How to Write a Financial Statement	63
	• How to Write a Balance Sheet	71
	• How to Make a Balance Sheet for Accounting	79
	• How to Read a Balance Sheet	84
	• How to Write an Income Statement	91
	• How to Prepare a Profit and Loss Statement	98
	• How to Review a Financial Statement	105
	• Single-entry Bookkeeping	108
	• How to Convert Single Entry into Double Entry	110
Chapter 4	**Skills for Becoming an Auditor**	**113**
	• Auditor	113
	• How to Become an Auditor	116
	• How to Audit	126
	• How to Perform a Basic Accounting Audit	132
	• How to Become a Certified Internal Auditor	139
	• How to Write an Audit Report	149
	• How to Become a Night Auditor	156
	• How to Gather Audit Evidence	161

- How to Become a Premium Audit Manager 169
- How to Prepare for a Workers Compensation Audit 170
- External Auditor 177

Chapter 5 **Auditing Processes** **178**
- How to Conduct an Operational Audit 178
- How to Conduct a Successful Audit Program 179
- How to Perform an Internal Audit 180
- How to Conduct a Quality Audit 182
- How to Develop an Effective Compliance Audit Process 183
- How to Conduct Tax Audit 184
- How to Conduct a Financial Audit 185
- How to Conduct Investigative Audit 186

Permissions

Index

Preface

Bookkeeping and auditing are important areas of accounting. Bookkeeping refers to recording of financial transactions. A bookkeeper is entrusted with the day-to-day record of financial transactions of a business. Maintaining records of receipts, sales, purchases and payments is a principal functional responsibility of a bookkeeper. An independent examination of accounts, books, statutory records and documents to ascertain if all financial statements and non-financial disclosures present a fair view of the organization is known as an audit. The auditor obtains evidence, evaluates them and formulates an opinion regarding the collected material. This book is compiled in such a manner, that it will provide in-depth knowledge about the theory and practice of bookkeeping and auditing. It presents these complex subjects in the most comprehensible and easy to understand language. Coherent flow of topics, student-friendly language and extensive use of examples make this book an invaluable source of knowledge.

Given below is the chapter wise description of the book:

Chapter 1- The process of recording financial transactions as a process of accounting is referred to as bookkeeping. All financial and non-financial disclosures are independently examined for authenticity in an audit. This chapter discusses in detail the theory and practice of bookkeeping and auditing and also explores why one should consider a career in bookkeeping and auditing.

Chapter 2- A bookkeeper is entrusted with the responsibility of recording everyday financial activities occurring in a business, and examining records such as purchases, payments and receipts. Some of the skills required for the profile of a bookkeeper are data entry skills, communication skills, good organization skills, attention to detail, etc. The topics elaborated in this chapter explore these skills for a successful career as a freelance or full-time bookkeeper, and also explores the ways to start a freelance bookkeeping and payroll service, etc.

Chapter 3- A bookkeeper is responsible for recording all cash and credit transactions in the appropriate daybook, customer ledger, supplier's ledger or general ledger. Bookkeeping involves a number of processes such as writing an accounting ledger, a general ledger, writing a balance sheet, reading a balance sheet, writing an income statement, preparing a profit and loss statement, reviewing a financial statement, etc. Such bookkeeping processes have been extensively covered in this chapter for a detailed understanding of bookkeeping.

Chapter 4- Some of the key skills required of an auditor include among others excellent problem-solving skills, a strong aptitude for mathematics, an understanding of finance, strong IT skills, interpersonal and communication skills, etc. An auditor should be able to examine financial control systems, analyze spreadsheet data, gauge financial risks, check records and reports for reliability, etc. Auditors consistently need to master or improve upon these core competencies for success in this domain. This chapter includes some vital topics such as performing a basic accounting audit, writing an audit report, preparing for a workers compensation audit, etc.

Chapter 5- This chapter explores the varied auditing processes, such as conducting an operational audit, conducting an audit program, performing an internal audit, conducting a tax audit, developing an effective compliance audit process, etc. These topics will enable an easy understanding of the processes involved in auditing.

At the end, I would like to thank all those who dedicated their time and efforts for the successful completion of this book. I also wish to convey my gratitude towards my friends and family who supported me at every step.

Harry Watts

CHAPTER

1

An Introduction to Bookkeeping and Auditing

The process of recording financial transactions as a process of accounting is referred to as bookkeeping. All financial and non-financial disclosures are independently examined for authenticity in an audit. This chapter discusses in detail the theory and practice of bookkeeping and auditing and also explores why one should consider a career in bookkeeping and auditing.

Bookkeeping

Bookkeeping involves the recording, on a daily basis, of a company's financial transactions. With proper bookkeeping, companies are able to track all information on its books to make key operating, investing, and financing decisions.

Bookkeepers are individuals who manage all financial data for companies. Without bookkeepers, companies would not be aware of their current financial position, as well as the transactions that occur within the company.

Accurate bookkeeping is also crucial to external users, which include investors, financial institutions, or the government that need access to reliable information to make better investment or lending decisions. Simply put, the entire economy relies on accurate and reliable bookkeeping for both internal and external users.

Importance of Bookkeeping

Proper bookkeeping gives companies a reliable measure of their performance. It also provides information on general strategic decisions and a benchmark for its revenue and income goals. In short, once a business is up and running, spending extra time and money on maintaining proper records is critical.

Many small companies don't actually hire full-time accountants to work for them because the costs are usually higher. Instead, small companies generally hire a bookkeeper or outsource the job to a professional firm. One important thing to note here is that many people who intend to start a new business sometimes overlook the importance of matters such as keeping records of every penny spent.

The Accrual vs Cash Basis of Accounting

In order to properly implement bookkeeping, companies need to first choose which basis of accounting they will follow. Companies can choose between two basic accounting methods: the cash basis of accounting or the accrual basis of accounting. The difference between these types of accounting is based on when you, the company, actually record the sale (money inflow) or purchase (money outflow) in the books.

Types of Bookkeeping

Traditional bookkeeping was performed using one of two systems. Accountants and bookkeepers used the systems to manually calculate company books and present financial statements in accordance with federal regulations. The two main systems still exist in today's digital era, but it's much easier to perform bookkeeping tasks for your company on the computer than by hand. Many business owners opt to do their own bookkeeping or outsource the duty to off-site accounting professionals.

Single-Entry System

The single-entry bookkeeping system is used for businesses that have minimal or uncomplicated transactions. This system records cash sales and business expenses that are paid when incurred. This system is not traditionally used for businesses that have accounts receivable, accounts payable or many capital transactions. Bookkeeping entries under this system don't match transactions to corresponding accounts, which can make tracing revenues and expenses more difficult. In essence, the single-entry system consists of a cash sales journal, a cash disbursements journal and your bank statements. An entry is made to the sales journal when revenue is received, and an entry is made to the disbursement journal when an expense is paid. Your journal entries should reconcile with your bank account transactions.

Double-Entry System

Double-entry bookkeeping systems are used for businesses that routinely have more complex transactions. Companies that collect income through accounts receivable and receive merchandise and inventory on credit are better-suited for this method. This system posts single transactions as an income or expense item, then creates a second entry to trace the transaction to a corresponding account. For example, if you receive income from a customer, the revenue is posted as income and also traced to the customer's account. In the event you are audited or need to know where income and expense payments generated, you'll have a paper trail to find the information quickly. This system uses debits and credits, which is the accountant's language of increases and decreases to each account affected by your transactions.

Bookkeeping Software

Many small-business owners use bookkeeping software to keep track of financial activities. Programs such as Quickbooks and Sage -- formerly Peachtree -- use the double-entry bookkeeping system, but you won't necessarily need to be well versed in the method to use the software. These programs are relatively user-friendly and prompt you to enter information to complete and post your transactions. Various versions of the software exist, ranging from basic to professional capacities, and you can purchase the software in desktop, online or cloud versions.

Virtual Bookkeeping

If the whole idea of single-entry and double-entry bookkeeping methods makes you queasy, you might benefit from virtual bookkeeping services. A virtual bookkeeper eliminates the need for expensive CPA fees or an in-house bookkeeping employee. Most virtual bookkeepers accept your sales invoices, expense receipts and payroll ledgers electronically. The bookkeeper posts your transactions to appropriate journals and ledgers, and emails you a copy of your reports. Virtual bookkeepers are typically CPAs or degreed accountants who tend to have lower fees than private CPA firms.

Auditing

Auditing is the process of assessment and ascertaining of financial, operational, and strategic goals and processes in organizations to determine whether they are in compliance with the stated principles in addition to them being in conformity with organizational and more importantly, regulatory requirements. Indeed, among the objectives of auditing as mentioned above, conformance with regulatory norms and rules and regulations is indeed one of the drivers behind auditing and historically and traditionally, has been the main reason why organizations get their financial statements, operational process, and strategic imperatives audited.

Types of Audits

Among the various types of audits, financial audits are the most popular followed by operational and strategic audits and in addition to the emerging practice of IT (Information Technology) audits. Moreover, auditing as a process has now become so routine and compulsory worldwide that organizations spend quite some time getting their books of accounts and processes audited by both internal and external auditors.

Internal Audits

Internal audits refer to the audits done by employees and stakeholders within the organizations with a view to evaluate and assess whether the organization is following the internal processes, norms, rules, and regulations in addition to determining whether it is in compliance with the regulatory norms.

Indeed, internal audits are sometimes the first checkpoints for organizations to determine whether their books of accounts, operational processes, and IT infrastructure and security protocols are in order with both the internal objectives, strategic imperatives, and external regulatory requirements.

Having said that, it must be noted that the reason why internal audits are not accorded more importance over external audits is that since they are being performed by employees and individuals within the organizations, the apparent lack of objectivity and thoroughness apart from a tendency to "cover things up" means that often, external audits are considered more trustworthy.

1. External Audits

   External audits are done by independent and third party agencies and companies that are especially tasked with assessing and evaluating an organizations' compliance with the regulatory norms.

   Further, some organizations also hire external auditors to "hold a mirror to themselves" in the sense that any deficiencies and irregularities can be found that are otherwise not "visible" to the senior leadership and management during the course of conducting the everyday operational business.

   Moreover, external audits are also mandatory due to regulatory and compliance reasons as well as due to the shareholder requirements which mandate that external audits need to be done annually, quarterly, and half yearly to be presented in the Annual General Meetings, and meetings of the Board of Directors.

   In addition, external audits might also be required in case of contingencies wherein the regulators who suspect that "something is amiss" in the companies might mandate those companies to be audited by independent and third party auditors to ascertain the "true picture" of the finances and operational details of those companies.

2. Financial Audits

   As mentioned earlier, financial audits are the most common form of audits for various reasons including the fact that businesses exist to make money and return profits and generate wealth for their shareholders. This means that investors and other stakeholders must know whether the businesses are being run properly so that their capital is safe and generating the stated returns.

   Moreover, financial audits are also the most common forms of audits since any discrepancies in the books of accounts reflects the mismanagement of the companies in addition to finance affecting almost all operational and strategic areas of the companies' and their businesses.

   In addition, financial audits are also the first point of evaluation as to whether the companies are stating the truth and whether they are hiding or covering up some aspect that can be uncovered and revealed in a forensic audit.

3. Strategic, Operational, and IT Audits

   Having said that, there are other types of audits such as operational, strategic, and IT audits that have become popular in recent years mainly due to the increasing complexity of organizational processes as well as the IT infrastructure and the fast paced external marketplace which needs an evaluation of whether the organizations are aligning their internal processes and strategies with that of the external strategic drivers and imperatives.

   In addition, IT audits are being sought to assess and evaluate the readiness of the organizations'

IT infrastructure and systems and IT processes to meet the stated goals and objectives in addition to being able to withstand IT risks and security breaches. Indeed, with the increase in the nature, type, and variety of IT risks as well as the increasing complexity of the IT infrastructure, IT audits have now become as commonplace as financial and operational audits because both internal and external stakeholders need to know whether the organization's IT infrastructure is up to the mark and whether it is capable of meeting the stated goals and objectives.

Internal & External Audits: First-, Second-, and Third-party Audits

- A first-party audit is performed within an organization to measure its strengths and weaknesses against its own procedures or methods and/or against external standards adopted by (voluntary) or imposed on (mandatory) the organization. A first-party audit is an internal audit conducted by auditors who are employed by the organization being audited but who have no vested interest in the audit results of the area being audited.
- A second-party audit is an external audit performed on a supplier by a customer or by a contracted organization on behalf of a customer. A contract is in place, and the goods or services are being, or will be, delivered. Second-party audits are subject to the rules of contract law, as they are providing contractual direction from the customer to the supplier. Second-party audits tend to be more formal than first-party audits because audit results could influence the customer's purchasing decisions.
- A third-party audit is performed by an audit organization independent of the customer-supplier relationship and is free of any conflict of interest. Independence of the audit organization is a key component of a third-party audit. Third-party audits may result in certification, registration, recognition, an award, license approval, a citation, a fine, or a penalty issued by the third-party organization or an interested party.

Purposes of Audits

An auditor may specialize in types of audits based on the audit purpose, such as to verify compliance, conformance, or performance. Some audits have special administrative purposes such as auditing documents, risk, or performance or following up on completed corrective actions.

Performance versus Compliance/Conformance Audits

Various authors use the following terms to describe an audit purpose beyond compliance and conformance: value-added assessments, management audits, added value auditing, and continual improvement assessment. The purpose of these audits goes beyond traditional compliance and conformance audits. The audit purpose relates to organization performance. Audits that determine compliance and conformance are not focused on good or poor performance. Yet performance is an important concern for most organizations.

A key difference between compliance/conformance audits and audits designed to promote improvement is the collection of audit evidence related to organization performance versus evidence to verify conformance or compliance to a standard or procedure. An organization may conform to its procedures for taking orders, but if every order is subsequently changed two or three times, management may have cause for concern and want to rectify the inefficiency.

Follow-up Audit

A product, process, or system audit may have findings that require correction and corrective action. Since most corrective actions cannot be performed at the time of the audit, the audit program manager may require a follow-up audit to verify that corrections were made and corrective actions were taken. Due to the high cost of a single-purpose follow-up audit, it is normally combined with the next scheduled audit of the area. However, this decision should be based on the importance and risk of the finding.

An organization may also conduct follow-up audits to verify preventive actions were taken as a result of performance issues that may be reported as opportunities for improvement. Other times organizations may forward identified performance issues to management for follow-up.

4 Phases of an Audit

1. Audit preparation – Audit preparation consists of everything that is done in advance by interested parties, such as the auditor, the lead auditor, the client, and the audit program manager, to ensure that the audit complies with the client's objective. The preparation stage of an audit begins with the decision to conduct the audit. Preparation ends when the audit itself begins.

2. Audit performance – The performance phase of an audit is often called the fieldwork. It is the data-gathering portion of the audit and covers the time period from arrival at the audit location up to the exit meeting. It consists of activities including on-site audit management, meeting with the auditee, understanding the process and system controls and verifying that these controls work, communicating among team members, and communicating with the auditee.

3. Audit reporting – The purpose of the audit report is to communicate the results of the investigation. The report should provide correct and clear data that will be effective as a management aid in addressing important organizational issues. The audit process may end when the report is issued by the lead auditor or after follow-up actions are completed.

4. Audit follow-up and closure – According to ISO 19011, clause 6.6, "The audit is completed when all the planned audit activities have been carried out, or otherwise agreed with the audit client." Clause 6.7 of ISO 19011 continues by stating that verification of follow-up actions may be part of a subsequent audit.

Reasons to Consider a Career in Bookkeeping and Auditing

You Control Your Career

The roles and responsibilities of a bookkeeper differ from accountants. Although the two have common goals, they primarily operate in different stages of the financial cycle. Both career pathways are essential in the world of finance.

If you start your career in bookkeeping, you can choose where and how quickly you progress.

Bookkeepers can also choose to work part-time or full-time to suit their needs. Longer work days are common around tax time and the end of financial year. Usually, bookkeepers work regular Monday - Friday business hours.

High Earning Potential

Earning a steady salary can be a great source of comfort for individuals in today's economy. Bookkeepers earn a solid income which grows with years of experience. The average salary of a bookkeeper in Australia is $55,000 a year. You can also easily transition into higher paid roles within the sector. For those who are dreaming of earning a salary that offers you the chance to fulfil lifelong aspirations such as travelling and buying a house, you should consider a career in bookkeeping.

Technological Skills are a Must

Many bookkeeping jobs involve a number of technical duties and often require knowledge of a variety of computer programs and systems. Strong computer skills are required as many bookkeeping functions have moved to cloud-based software like MYOB and Xero. Although the roles and responsibilities of a bookkeeper will still require you to be able to make calculations manually to ensure accuracy, having a grasp of IT related skills to the accounting field will put you ahead of the job competition.

Digital programs are used in bookkeeping to make the job easier. Once you have landed a role in bookkeeping, you can sharpen up your computer skills. However, most programs will be intuitive and should not cause you too much trouble.

Passionate Career

Anyone with a love of numbers will find bookkeeping to be the ideal career pathway. The roles and responsibilities of a bookkeeper require a great amount of attention to detail and patience. If you are not a strong multi-tasker, there is no need to worry. Bookkeeping generally requires you to focus on one financial situation at a time so that your work is accurate.

If you are a social person, you should consider a career in bookkeeping. Day-to-day interactions with clients ensure that you can be closely involved with a wide range of people. On the other hand, if you find that you are more of an introverted person, there are still plenty of opportunities for you in bookkeeping as well. The diversity of the role makes it a great choice for personalities of all types.

CHAPTER 2

Skills for Becoming a Bookkeeper

A bookkeeper is entrusted with the responsibility of recording everyday financial activities occurring in a business, and examining records such as purchases, payments and receipts. Some of the skills required for the profile of a bookkeeper are data entry skills, communication skills, good organization skills, attention to detail, etc. The topics elaborated in this chapter explore these skills for a successful career as a freelance or full-time bookkeeper, and also explores the ways to start a freelance bookkeeping and payroll service, etc.

Bookkeeper

The bookkeeper position creates financial transactions and creates financial reports from that information. The creation of financial transactions includes posting information to accounting journals or accounting software from such source documents as invoices to customers, cash receipts, and supplier invoices. The bookkeeper also reconciles accounts to ensure their accuracy.

Principal Accountabilities:

1. Purchase supplies and equipment as authorized by management.
2. Monitor office supply levels and reorder as necessary.
3. Tag and monitor fixed assets.
4. Pay supplier invoices in a timely manner.
5. Take all reasonable discounts on supplier invoices.
6. Pay any debt as it comes due for payment.
7. Monitor debt levels and compliance with debt covenants.
8. Issue invoices to customers.
9. Collect sales taxes from customers and remit them to the government.
10. Ensure that receivables are collected promptly.
11. Record cash receipts and make bank deposits.
12. Conduct a monthly reconciliation of every bank account.
13. Conduct periodic reconciliations of all accounts to ensure their accuracy.
14. Maintain the petty cash fund.
15. Issue financial statements.
16. Provide information to the external accountant who creates the company's financial statements.

17. Assemble information for external auditors for the annual audit.
18. Calculate and issue financial analysis of the financial statements.
19. Maintain an orderly accounting filing system.
20. Maintain the chart of accounts.
21. Maintain the annual budget.
22. Calculate variances from the budget and report significant issues to management.
23. Comply with local, state, and federal government reporting requirements.
24. Process payroll in a timely manner.
25. Provide clerical and administrative support to management as requested.

How to be a Bookkeeper

1. Start with an Internship

Many bookkeeping and accounting offices are willing to let high school or college students work part-time as interns. They get help with their jobs, and you get a first-hand look at what it's like to work as a bookkeeper.

During an internship, you'll probably learn about the computer programs the company uses, as well as how the company maintains accurate records and stays on top of the latest regulations.

2. Get Familiar with Accounting Software

One of the best ways to learn what it takes to become a bookkeeper is to study accounting software and get a feel for how it works. You can also always talk to a bookkeeper in person for more hands-on learning, too.

Knowing how to use programs like a pay stub generator is also helpful in making you a valuable bookkeeper. These tools streamline the bookkeeping process and help you make sure everyone gets paid on time.

3. Consider Additional Education

Some employers want their bookkeepers to have at least an associate's degree. Look at postings for jobs near you and find out if that's the case for businesses in your area. If so, it might be worth the investment to go back to school so that you can make yourself more marketable.

4. Get Certified

After you've worked as a bookkeeper for at least two years, you can become a Certified Bookkeeper through the American Institute of Professional Bookkeepers.

To receive this certification, you need to pass a four-part exam and adhere to a code of ethics.

Being a Certified Bookkeeper will open you up to a whole new level of bookkeeping jobs, with higher pay and other benefits. It's worth doing if you think bookkeeping is the career for you.

5. Get Licensed

After becoming a Certified Bookkeeper, you can go on to become a licensed Certified Public Bookkeeper.

This distinction comes from the National Association of Certified Public Bookkeepers. To attain it, you'll need to take 24 hours of continuing professional education classes every year.

How to Bookkeep

Part 1. Establishing a System

1. Decide what type of system to use. The most important part of bookkeeping is being consistent. You don't want to lose receipts, forget to record transactions, or record the same transaction twice, as this could cause a misrepresentation of your business's financial health. The simplest way to avoid these errors in by establishing a consistent system for both recording transactions in journals and entering them into the ledger.

This system can be as complicated as a wired-in cash register that feeds into accounting software or as simple as a box full of receipts and notes. This will depend on the amount of transactions your company does on a daily or weekly basis.

2. Use accounting software. The simplest way to ensure that your transactions are recorded reliably is to invest in an accounting program like QuickBooks, FreshBooks, or Expensify. These will take a lot of the guesswork out of recording different types of transactions and present your information clearly. Many of these programs are available for free or on as a free trial for a limited time.

3. Use a spreadsheet. For a more manual system, try setting up a spreadsheet to record transactions. This can be done either manually, with physical transaction journals, or on the computer

with a spreadsheet program. The formatting of these journals is up to you, but it should include the following, at minimum:

- Supplier's/buyer's name
- Account number
- Expense/revenue type (e.g. office supplies, raw materials)
- Date the invoice was received/created
- Amount owed/paid

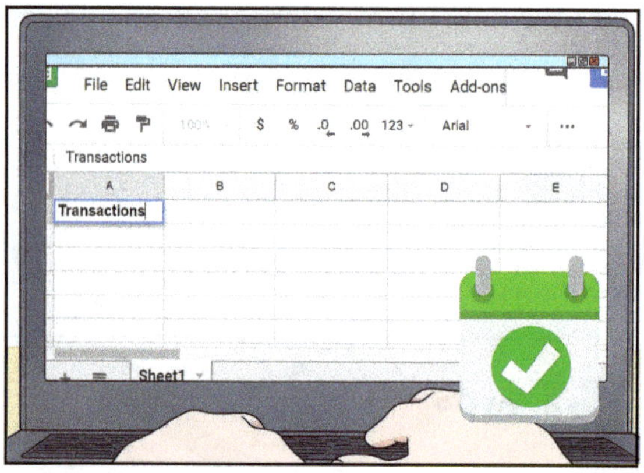

4. Be consistent. For any system you use, be sure to enter your transaction data on a regular basis and in the same way each time. This is to be sure that transactions are not overlooked and that you have the most up to date picture of your business's financial health. In addition, it is a good idea to establish a regular schedule for transferring information from the journals to the ledger, perhaps on a weekly or monthly basis.

Part 2. Recording Transactions Properly

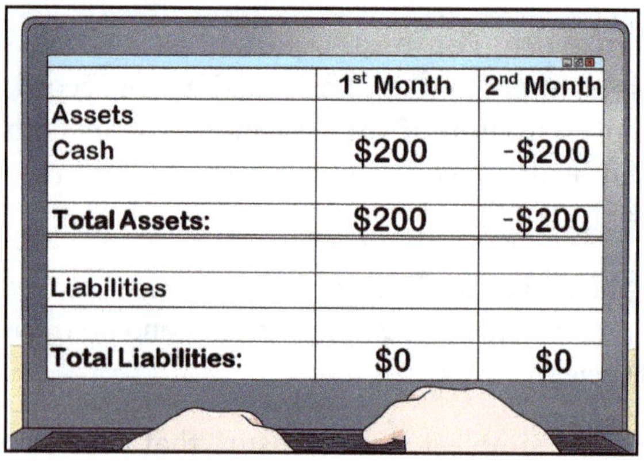

Use the same accounting method for all entries. The two types of accounting are the cash and accrual accounting methods. In essence, the cash method records transactions when actual cash changes hands, like when a customer pays for an item or when you pay for an expense. The accrual method, however, accounts for transactions when that transaction occurs, for example when expenses are incurred or when a customers buys an item (but not necessarily when money changes hands for the transaction). Which method you choose will depend on your own goals and business strategies.

2. Compare the two accounting methods. The cash method of accounting is more commonly used in small businesses because it gives an accurate representation of the cash balance of the company. As the business grows, however, it may become less important to know the exact cash balance of the company and focus instead on its current health. This is where the accrual method comes in. By tracking expenses when they occur and revenues when they are earned, rather than paid for, the accrual method negates the effects of payment delays in determining the financial health of the company.

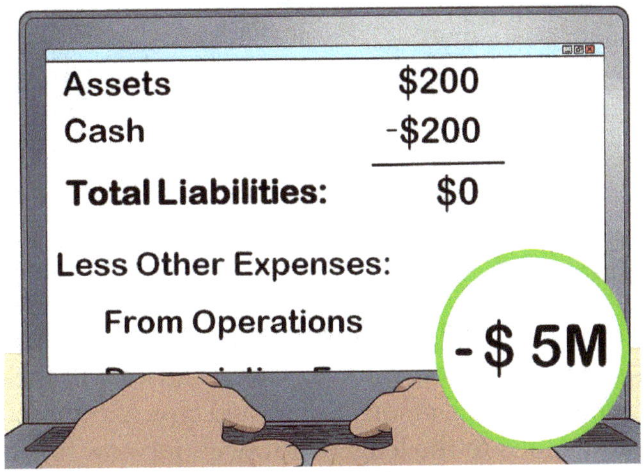

3. Decide on which method to use. Legally, a company may choose either accounting method as long that company has less than $5 million in revenue each year or, if it sells products to the public, has less than $1 million in gross receipts (all revenues). Any company with revenues over those levels is required, by law, to use the accrual method.

4. Use double-entry bookkeeping. Many small businesses make the mistake of using single-entry bookkeeping. That is, they only record transactions as movements of money to or from a single account. However, every business transaction takes place in at least two accounts, and must be recorded as such for accuracy. This is called double-entry bookkeeping. This allows you to see exactly where your money is coming from and where it's going.

- For example, a purchase of inventory using cash would be recorded as an increase in inventory and a decrease in the cash account. Alternately, a sale of that inventory to a customer paying in credit would be recorded as a decrease in inventory and an increase in accounts receivable.
- In the world of accounting, these would be recorded using the official terms, as debits and credits to various accounts. As a bookkeeper, though, it is most important that you use a consistent system that makes sense to you.

5. Record transactions in journals. At first, transactions need only be entered into daily or weekly journals, depending on your transaction volume. These entries will include information on the transaction, including the buyer/seller, amount, date, and type of transaction. Later, this information will be categorized and added to the ledger. However, for now it is only important to record the information for later use. Entries should be made according the company's chosen accounting method (cash or accrual).

- The introduction of accounting software has made the two-step process of journals and ledgers almost obsolete. The software will automatically update the ledger, making the process one of simply inputting transactions as they occur. However, some businesses still choose to use the journal-ledger method.

Part 3. Posting Transactions to a Ledger

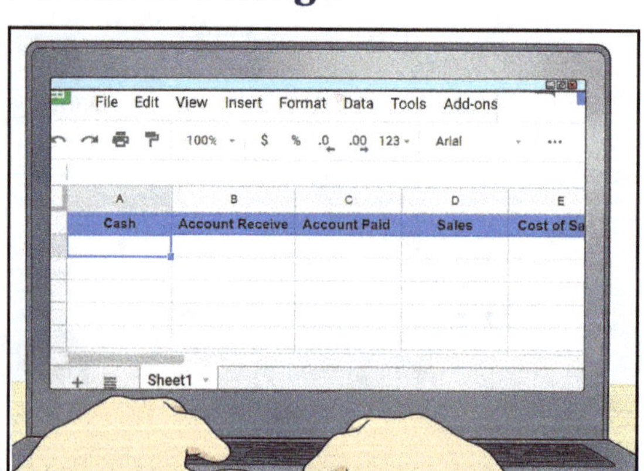

1. Separate transactions into accounts. The best way to track your transactions is to separate them into different accounts within the ledger. By starting out with set accounts and adding or subtracting from them with each transaction, you gain a clearer picture of where money is coming in and

going. These accounts can be as generic as sales or as specific certain types of inventory. For example, it may be reasonable for an auto garage to reserve an entire account for oil inventory. Accounts will vary between businesses, but at minimum should cover the following:

- Cash
- Accounts Receivable (money due from customers paying on credit).
- Accounts Payable (money you owe to suppliers).
- Sales (the revenue you make from primary operations).
- Inventory
- Cost of sales (supplies you buy for production or your business).
- Payroll Expenses (wages).
- Owners' Equity (the amount that owners have put into the business).
- Retained Earnings (profits reinvested in the company).

2. Post transactions regularly. How often you post transaction to the ledger from the journals will depend on your transaction volume. It can be daily, weekly, or even monthly. However, this should be done consistently to ensure that you are not suddenly overwhelmed with work at the end of an accounting period. Again, accounting software will help you stay up-to-date on these processes.

3. Analyze your ledger accounts. Ledger accounts are mainly useful for quantifying the financial health of the company. While true financial reports are best left to professional accountants, any-

one can compare ledger accounts to create simple comparisons or reports. For example, compare sales to expenses to get a general idea of how your company has fared recently. Obviously, if sales are higher than expenses, you are making a profit. For more complex reports, turn to an accountant or accounting program.

How to do Bookkeeping for a Small Business

Part 1. Setting Up Your Accounts Payable

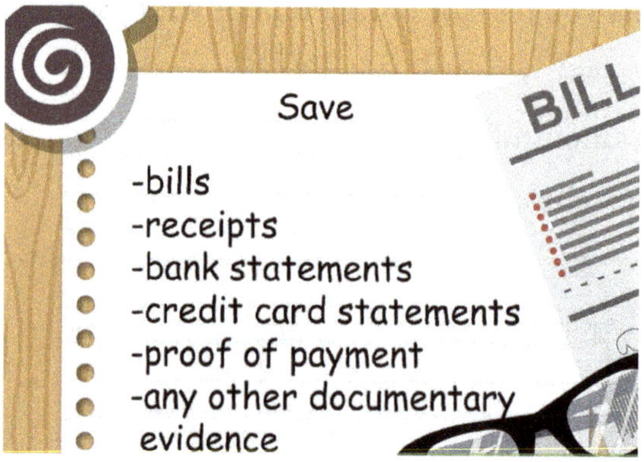

1. Save proof of business expenses. Accounts payable is the amount of money you owe other people for business expenses. If you buy inventory or supplies, then you'll need to collect proof of the expense. You'll also need this information later at tax time. Save the following:

- bills
- receipts
- bank statements
- credit card statements
- proof of payment
- any other documentary evidence

2. Set up a spreadsheet or ledger. You'll need create an electronic spreadsheet or ledger on a piece

of paper. If you don't want to do this yourself, there is bookkeeping software you can purchase that will make bookkeeping easy.

- Think about moving to an automated system when you're receiving more than two bills a day or your expenses are increasing rapidly.

3. Create columns for necessary information. You'll include the following information on your spreadsheet or ledger, so create a column for each:

- supplier's name
- account number
- type of expense (e.g., office supplies, professional services, etc.)
- date you received the invoice
- amount you owe

4. Post information daily. It's important not to overlook accounts payable and forget to include them on your spreadsheet. Get in the habit of posting information daily.

- If you have few expenses, then you might want to post only weekly or monthly, but it's key that you remember to develop a routine.

5. Pay your bills in a timely fashion. Remember to pay bills frequently—on a weekly basis is ideal. Don't wait until the due date. Instead, give yourself a few days in advance of the deadline.

- Paying bills early is a good way to maintain effective relations with your vendors.
- However, if you've been hired by a business to work as a bookkeeper, then paying on time is a necessity for maintaining your job.

Part 2. Setting up your Accounts Receivable

1. Create an invoice template. You want your invoice to be clear so that clients will pay as quickly as possible. Include the following information on your invoice:

- your business contact information
- your business logo (if applicable)
- clear payment terms, such as "payment is due in 30 days of invoice date"
- detail about the specifics of your service
- hours worked
- the name a check should be made out to (particularly important if you operate under a fictitious business name)

2. Save proof of payment and other documents. Just as you document your expenses, also document your accounts receivable. Hold onto the following, and create electronic copies if possible:

- invoices
- cancelled checks
- other proof of payment

3. Create a spreadsheet or ledger. You need something to enter your accounts receivable information onto. Choose a spreadsheet or a ledger book. Also consider using software. You can use the same software for accounts receivable that you use for accounts payable.

- If you are receiving 5-10 invoices a week, you should consider automating the system.

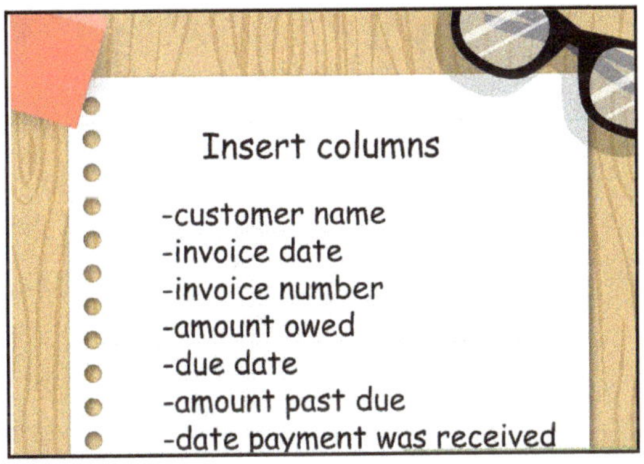

4. Insert columns for accounts receivable information. Set up columns for the following information on your spreadsheet or ledger:

- customer name
- invoice date
- invoice number
- amount owed
- due date
- amount past due
- date payment was received

5. Post information to your ledgers regularly. Get in the habit of staying on top of the amounts your customers owe you. You should post accounts receivable regularly, which will depend on the size of your business. The key is to get in a consistent habit so that you don't forget.

- If you're receiving multiple invoices a day, then posting daily is a good idea.
- However, if you have only a few big invoices a month, then you might want to post monthly or weekly.
- Nevertheless, if you're posting accounts payable daily, you should get in the habit of reviewing accounts receivable at the same time.

6. Follow up on late payments. A bookkeeper also needs to track down customers who haven't paid in a timely fashion. You'll need to send appropriate letters telling the client their bill is due.

- If you find clients aren't paying the business, you might want to talk with the owner about giving customers more options for making payment. For example, the business could accept credit cards.

Part 3. Documenting Petty Cash

1. Establish the starting balance. You can quickly lose track of where your petty cash has gone if you don't keep accurate records. Accordingly, start with an initial balance. Make it small enough that your employees won't feel tempted to steal from it but large enough that it can cover reasonable expenses.

- Most small businesses can get by with $50-200 in petty cash.

2. Require receipts. Keep careful records of what petty cash is spent on. Require your employees to provide receipts of all purchases made using petty cash. Have a folder where you store receipts, and get in the habit of organizing receipts on a weekly basis.

3. Create a log. You should also keep a log along with your receipts. You need the log because not

every purchase will have a receipt. On the log, record the amount taken from petty cash and what is was spent on. Enter the information immediately.

- For example, if you took $20 out to buy new pens for the office, you should enter the information as soon as you remove the money from the petty cash box. If you have money left over, then record that you are returning money to the petty cash box

4. Replenish by writing a check to yourself. This is a good way to document cash transfers. You can keep a copy of the cancelled check that shows which account you transferred money from. Don't just take cash from your own wallet and dump it in the petty cash box.

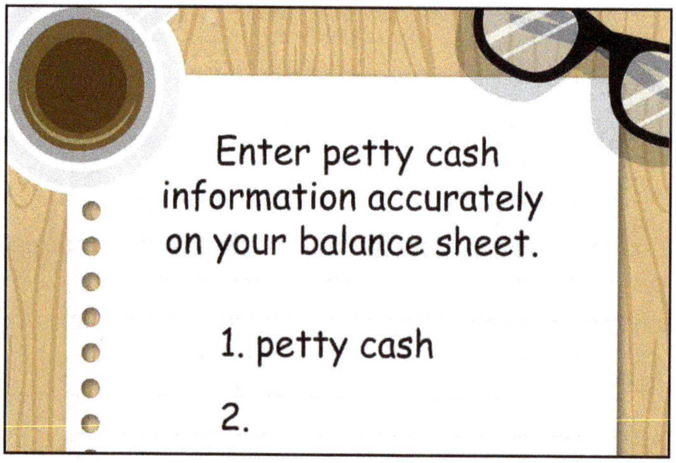

5. Enter petty cash information accurately on your balance sheet. Consider petty cash to be an asset on your financial statements. Don't neglect to accurately record it. Although the amounts may seem small, they can add up quickly for a small business.

Part 4. Reconciling your Accounts

1. Keep ledgers for all financial accounts. You may have several business bank accounts. For example, small businesses usually have a checking account to pay bills and a savings account to save up money to pay self-employment tax. You should also create a ledger or spreadsheet for each of your major accounts.

- Keeping this ledger will allow you to monitor the current state of your business. You won't have to wait for the monthly bank statement to see if your business is insolvent or thriving.

2. Reconcile your books. You need to make sure that your monthly recording of expenses is the same that shows up on your bank records. This means analyzing your bank statement and your accounts to make sure the same transactions appear on each.

- Reconciliation is a good way to catch mistakes—yours or the bank's. If the bank makes a mistake, you can contact them. Share whatever documentation you have (receipts, cancelled checks).
- You can also catch fraudulent activity with reconciliation. For example, an employee might have withdrawn money from the checking account without telling you.
- Perform reconciliation monthly. If you wait too long, it will be harder to reconcile. Also, you won't catch fraudulent transactions in a timely manner.

3. Meet with the accountant. You may need to meet with the company's accountant once a month to go over the books. The accountant can identify any recordings that are unclear or inaccurate, and you can talk about them.

How to Become a Freelance Bookkeeper

1. Skills Needed to become a Freelance Bookkeeper

While going through your application, the first thing the employer will assess is the portfolio of skills or resume attached to it. The portfolio of skills is extremely important and, therefore, proper attention must be given in its formulation.

You cannot randomly add any kind of skill, which has no relevance to the job of bookkeeping whatsoever, and thus, read whatever is mentioned below carefully and incorporate the same in the portfolio.

- Technology educated: Technology has redefined everything that surrounds us and without it, we can hardly imagine life. Technology affects efficiency and when it comes to bookkeeping, efficiency is a must-have. Thus, if you wish to become a bookkeeper, you must work on your computer skills and be well acquainted with utilities such as spread sheets, MS office, the Internet, etc.
- Communication skills: A bookkeeper is not a lone worker in the account's department of a company; he/she works in a team, and when working in a team, it becomes imperative to communicate. There your communication skills will play a key role in conveying your queries, reservations, and suggestions on the matter of data recording and, at times, interpretation.
- Accounting Education: This goes without saying that without substantial knowledge of accounting, there is no chance. You must not only be well-versed with the principles and concepts of accounting but also be able to put them into real-time use.
- Organization: If you are a bookkeeper, you will have to organize the data anyway. You may often come across myriad of unrelated and unrefined data, and it is up to you to determine the data and organize it as per the guidelines of the company.

2. Work Opportunities for Freelance Bookkeeper

Most organizations—whether public or private—require bookkeepers. Data inflow is usually heavy and without any organization and the assistance of bookkeepers, everything will go simply haywire.

While the work opportunities are plenty, a more important question should be asked as to how to keep a track on the availability of jobs.

The answer is freelance websites. These websites are hoards of opportunities, and one can have a 24×7 access to these through simple formalities—the creation of a profile, submission of a portfolio of skills and customization of job searches. You will, then, receive filtered notifications and can, accordingly, submit applications. Examples of such websites include linkedin.com, letsintern.com, worknhire.com, etc.

How to Start a Freelance Bookkeeping and Payroll Service

Nearly every company needs bookkeeping and payroll services. Accurate bookkeeping and payroll services are important to the successful operation of a company. Some companies cannot afford to hire staff permanently, so they employ the services of freelance bookkeepers. Other small companies do not need permanent staff because of their small financial requirements. If you like working with numbers, consider starting a bookkeeping and payroll company. As a freelance bookkeeper and payroll service provider, you set your own prices, take on as many clients as you desire and establish the services you wish to provide.

1. Choose the services you desire to offer clients. Select bookkeeping services to offer clients, such as accounts receivable, accounts payable, bank reconciliation, payroll and financial report preparation. Offer additional services if you desire, including audit preparation, loan packaging, business plans and accounting software training.

2. Seek voluntary certification. Obtain certification from the American Institute of Professional Bookkeepers or the National Association of Certified Public Bookkeepers (NACPB) after meeting eligibility requirements. You can apply for bookkeeping and payroll certifications with NACPB. You must pass an examination covering bookkeeping concepts before receiving certification.

3. Purchase bookkeeping and payroll software. Choose software you can customize to your clients' needs, that's easy to use and inexpensive. Verify that your computer meets the specifications of the software installation requirements. Obtain training in several accounting software programs to meet the needs of your clients.

4. Set your freelance rates. Call local bookkeeping and payroll companies to ask their prices, which will give you an idea of what to charge your clients. Decide whether to set an hourly rate or a flat monthly fee. Consider charging extra fees for mileage if you must travel to your clients' offices. Bookkeeping and payroll rates vary by region and professional experience. A bookkeeper with many years of experience typically charges more than a bookkeeper with little experience.

5. Join business organizations in your area and your local chamber of commerce. Introduce yourself to business owners and give a brief explanation of your business and the services you provide. Schedule an introductory meeting with individuals interested in your business. Explain your services in more detail, your bookkeeping and payroll processes and your fees. Sign a contract with clients interested in retaining your services.

6. Send your resume to employers looking for part-time bookkeepers. Follow up with a phone call if possible. Inform employers of the benefits of hiring a freelance bookkeeping and payroll service provider as opposed to an employee. As an independent contractor, clients do not provide you with health benefits and other fringe benefits or pay payroll taxes. Promote these cost-saving facts when you speak with them about the benefits of hiring a freelance bookkeeping and payroll service provider.

How to Obtain a Bookkeeping Certificate Online

Part 1. Studying for Certification

1. Gain at least 1 year of accounting or bookkeeping experience. The NBA requires that candidates for certification have 1 year of working in the accounting or bookkeeping field. This will help you learn hands-on applications of the fundamental information needed for your certification.

- The NBA doesn't distinguish between full-time and part-time experience in the field.

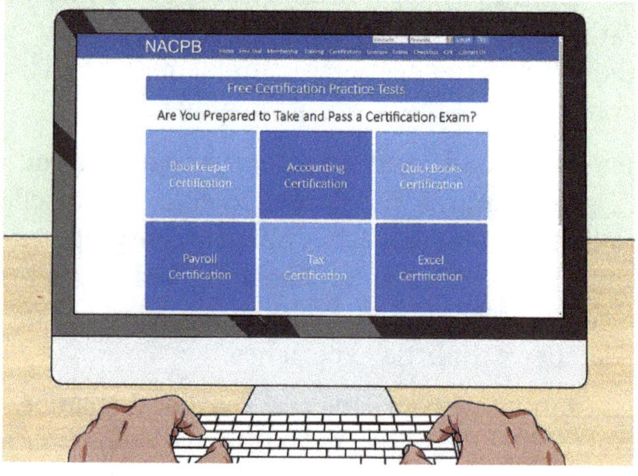

2. Take the online certification practice test. The practice test will tell you your current competency level and let you know if you're ready to take the certification exam. It covers the same topics as the certification exam.

- Visit http://certifiedpublicbookkeeper.org/free-certification-practice-tests.cfm and select "Bookkeeper Certification" to register to take the online practice test.
- As a general rule, if you pass the practice test, you're ready to take the certification exam. However, it doesn't hurt to brush up on your skills for a little bit before taking the exam.

3. Brush up on your study skills. If you've been in the workforce for a long time, you might have forgotten what it's like to study for an exam. If you didn't do well on the practice test, make a study plan and stick to it so that you can receive your certification.

- It will be helpful to have a notebook dedicated to your certification, where you can take notes and track your progress. This will help you decide the right time to take the exam.

4. Review common exam topics with teaching videos from the NACPB. The videos, which are free to members of the NACPB, include pre-lesson tests, instructional videos, and post-lesson quizzes. They're a great resource if you just need to brush up on some of your skills before taking the certification exam.

- The video quizzes also give you a good idea of the structure and wording of the questions on the certification exam.

5. Enroll in the Bookkeeping Certification program for a discount on the certification exam. The

online course from NACPB covers the information included in the certification exam in more depth than the free videos. The course is online, self-taught, and you can complete it at your own pace, and includes the price of the certification exam in the cost.

- This is a great option if you have minimal experience in hands-on bookkeeping. It gives you a variety of educational resources, including an online textbook, workbook, and study guides, as well as exercises and practice tests.
- Although the course is online, you have access to an instructor who can provide you with additional support.
- The cost of this program for non-members is $599 or $499 for members.
- There is an option for taking the accounting course that does not include the price of the exam, but the educational program is the best deal if you intend to take the certification exam.

Part 2. Taking the Certification Exam

1. Pay the $150 fee for access to the exam. If you've opted not to take the educational program that includes the exam, you will have to pay a fee before you take the test. Once you pay this fee, you have one year to take and pass the exam from the date of purchase.

- This fee is discounted to $100 for members of the NACPB.

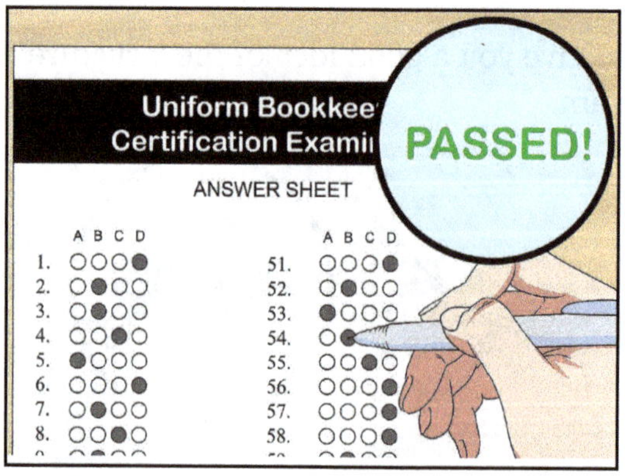

2. Pass the Uniform Bookkeeper Certification Examination by scoring at least 75%. The test is administered online and takes two hours to complete. This is exam is a comprehensive overview of many different topics in accounting and bookkeeping.

- The exam includes topics such as the language of business, adjustments, accounting for sales, cash, payroll, general journal and ledger keeping, accruals and deferrals, and many more.
- If you don't pass the exam, you can pay to retake the exam.

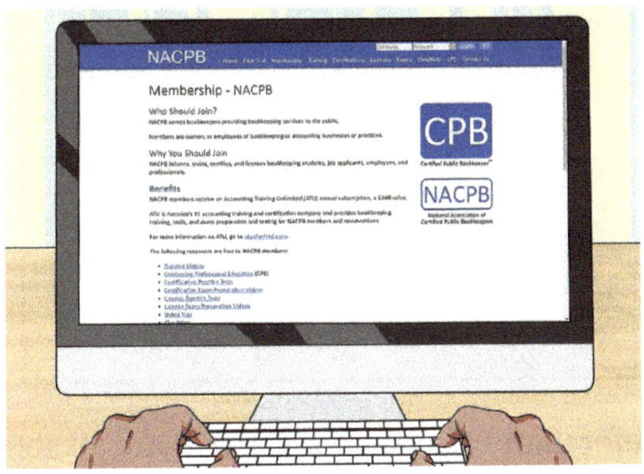

3. Join NACPB for discounts and further benefits of membership. Members receive discounts on courses, access to free educational videos and practice exams. If you're interested in getting a bookkeeping license in the future, membership includes resources that can prepare you for that process.

- Annual membership dues cost $100, but there is a 1-day free trial membership available that will give you access to member resources. After your free trial, you can decide whether membership is right for you.
- If you are in a position or are preparing to work in a business where you provide bookkeeping services to the public, you are eligible to be a member.

How to Study for a Bookkeeping Exam

Method 1. Taking Your Time

1. This method is to applied when you have sufficient time to read before the open book exam. The method emphasis the fact that open book exams are not the same as ordinary closed book exams

and thus would require a different study approach. Here are the steps that will guide you to prepare when you have sufficient time before the exam.

2. Start studying for exams beforehand as open book exams are all about how you retrieve or apply a concept and thus don't expect to find quick answers by reading the book or notes during the open book exam as your time will be limited.

3. Collect your Resources: Get your textbook, related reference materials and class notes (if you have any). If your teacher uses slides to teach than get your subject slides too to read. (A Computer will be required to read the slides or any other thing that can read slides/presentations).

4. Familiarize the Test Portion: Know your syllabus and tick the chapters for the exam. Now start with first chapter, Break up the chapter into co-headings. Now go through your slides for the first chapter in a quick succession and note down important formulas or points in pictorial manner and

in compact fashion so that you can easily revise and remember things positioning. You can also underline the important concepts and theories in the textbook for easy retrieval during revising. Maintain a notes book to note these down and number each page number which will help you when you create the easy retrieval guide index.

5. Start Preparing: Now you will find the textbook easier to read and you can skim through it and can focus on doing problems. Try remembering important formulas and concepts as it's always good to remember then just noting them down as it gives you a time advantage during the exams as you no longer have to search for the formulas and concepts. Practice by questioning yourself of what possible questions could be asked and how you would interpret it. Note down your mistakes to avoid them during the exam. Note down your mistakes, possible questions and interpretations in your notes book to get an advantage during the exam.

6. Organize your knowledge: Similarly study for other chapters and write down important points from both slides and book in pictorial manner (you can also include page numbers for key words). Maintain an easy retrieval guide index for easy accessing of concepts and formulas during the exam. Here is how to make an easy retrieval guide index:

- Firstly write the chapter name and number. Under the heading write down the important concepts and formulas and index the page numbers where they are available. This will allow a quick retrieval during exams.
- You can distinguish between concepts, headings, subheadings and formulas by designating some symbols to them which in turn will allow a quick specific retrieval. For example formulas can be given a star symbol and concepts can be given a flag symbol.

- Also index the Page numbers of notebook pages under the respective subject headings and write the page numbers in a different colored pen to help you realize that the point is present in your notes that you created. You can put a cross symbol besides the mistakes or possible danger points in your notes to help you stay alert on not making mistakes.

7. Now your chapter maps and mind is organized enough to write an open book exam.

Method 2. Cramming

1 This method is for those students who have insufficient time to prepare for open book exams. Though this method doesn't allow a full throttle performance that you could have achieved by Method-1, but still we will help you prepare for the best in a short amount of time. In this method we will be using a R-N-I-R approach (Read-Note-Index-Revise).

2. Collect your Resources: Get your textbook, related reference materials and class notes (if you

have any). If your teacher uses slides to teach than get your subject slides too to read. (A Computer will be required to read the slides or any other thing that can read slides/presentations)

3. Familiarize the Test Portion: Know your syllabus and tick the chapters for the exam. Check out the syllabus and consult your friends and teachers about chapters which are the most important to know for the exam. Prioritize your chapters based on their importance for the exam and start with the one at the top. Anyhow we will be reading all chapters so you need not worry much about prioritizing while reading, but this will help when it comes to revising as you never know what can happen in an open book exam.

4. Start Reading (R): Start reading your slides and notes to get a brief review about the concepts and formulas involved. After this you'll have an idea on what the subjects are about. Now go to your textbook and just skim for the important points and mark them. Books usually contain lots of explanations and stories so skimming is a good idea in order to save time.

5. Take Notes (N): Here notes' taking is very much different from the one in Method-1. In this step write down the summary of the chapters in a pictorial manner along with the page numbers

if possible which will in turn become the Indexing (I) part of your preparation. Pictorial representations will simply boost your preparation and will eventually fill up the lack of preparation time.

6. Revise (R): Now as you have organized your preparation, simply workout the old or previous year question papers. While a maintaining an exam environment as mentioned in "Final Call" step of Method-1. Check with the solutions released with the paper. Note your weak points and eradicate them by revising them again. In case you missed something in your Indexing then do note them after the trial test while studying. Reevaluate your performance and preparation by writing more such trial open book exams.

CHAPTER

3

Bookkeeping Processes

A bookkeeper is responsible for recording all cash and credit transactions in the appropriate day-book, customer ledger, supplier's ledger or general ledger. Bookkeeping involves a number of processes such as writing an accounting ledger, a general ledger, writing a balance sheet, reading a balance sheet, writing an income statement, preparing a profit and loss statement, reviewing a financial statement, etc. Such bookkeeping processes have been extensively covered in this chapter for a detailed understanding of bookkeeping.

How to Write an Accounting Ledger

Part 1. Recording Expenses in Journals

1. Know that a journal is a list of every transaction your company makes. An accounting journal records the details, date, and amount of all the money flowing in and out of your business. It is non-specific, meaning that you record everything in the journal no matter where the money is going. You must first post your transactions in a journal before your post them in a ledger.

- There are many computer programs, like Quicken, QuickBooks, and more, which will help your write journals and ledgers accurately and efficiently.

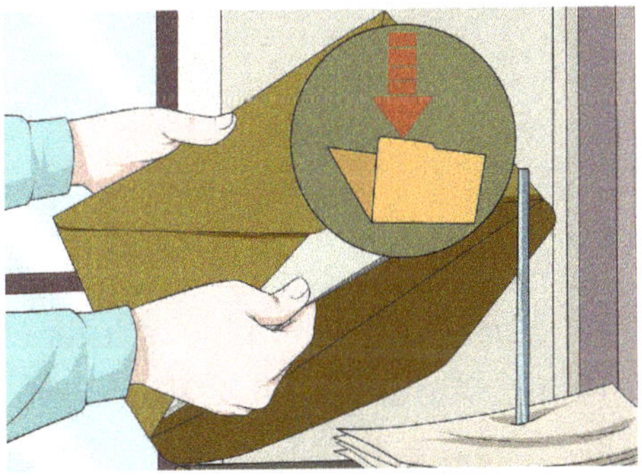

2. Save copies of all your business receipts, invoices, and debts. You need to have accurate docu-

mentation to create an accurate accounting journal and ledger, so save everything you have that relates to finances for later use.

- The sooner you log a transaction in your journal, the less likely it is to fall through the cracks and be forgotten.

3. Set up your journal page. Using a spreadsheet or a computer accounting program, begin a new journal page by dividing the page up into five columns:

- Date
- Account
- Description
- Reference Number
- Debit
- Credit

4. Record transactions the date that they occur. Under your "date" heading, mark when a transaction was made. You should have a journal for every type of interaction your business does. If you receive a $500 check for your business on April 20th, 2015, start the journal entry with 4/20/15.

- You need accurate dates for accurate bookkeeping. Find a time at least once a week to log all of your journal entries to make sure you don't lose any.

5. Categorize the "account" of the transaction. This is where the vocabulary of accounting is especially handy. Accounts are ways to think of how your money is being spent or earned. For example, the $500 check adds to your business's cash, so it would be labeled 4/20/15, Cash. Some of the most common accounts include:

- Cash: Money that your business has on hand. This is not necessarily hard cash. If someone writes your business a $500 check, for example, it would be an increase in cash.
- Accounts Payable: These are business expenses you owe. For example, if the $500 check you received is a loan, you need to note $500 under your accounts payable journal.
- Accounts Receivable: This is money that your business is owed.
- General Journal: This journal is essential to capture all weird or one-time transactions, like bad debts, inflation, selling equipment, etc.
- Sales: The the revenue generated by selling your business's product.
- Equipment, Wages, Land These three accounts, usually separate, detail the expenses needed to keep your business running.

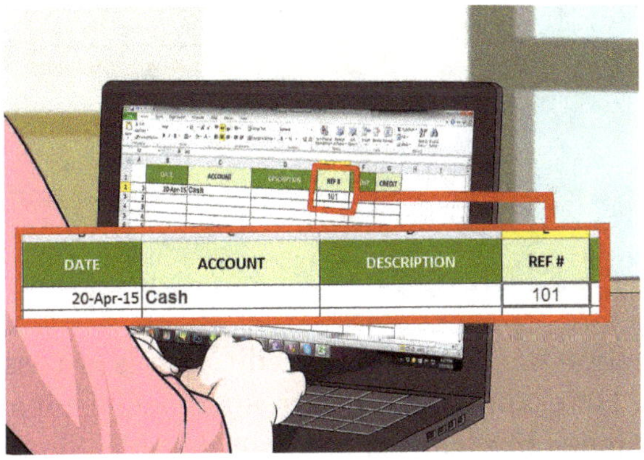

6. Assign each account a number for easy reference. This is usually referred to as you "chart of accounts." Usually, similar accounts are listed near each other, so you might label Wage Costs 501, Utility Costs 521, and Advertising Costs 531. This helps you easily order and reference you different accounts later on. For example, if you decide to label "Cash" as 101, then you can mark your check as 4/20/15, Cash, #501.

- The space between numbers (501 and 521) is so you can add new entries in between them. For example, if you are using physical books, or want to start a new journal every year, you might label "Wage Costs" as all account numbers 501-520, one for each of the next 20 years.

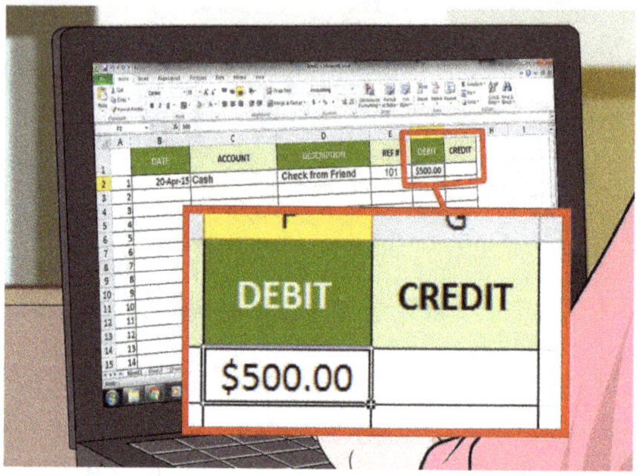

7. Record the details of your transaction. After listing the date, account, and reference number, briefly describe the transaction. This only needs to be enough information to accurately remind you where the money came from or why it was spent. With the check example, you would write 4/20/15, Cash, #501, Check from Friend. Some other examples of descriptions include:

- "Loan from Liberty Bank."
- "Money from tax return."
- "Sale of old oven."
- "Repairs to factory roof."

8. Note whether the transaction was a debit or a credit. Debits are assets, or things that increase the worth of your business. For example, if you earn $500, you list it as debit. Credits are expenses, or liabilities, of your business, like loans or accounts payable. Simply list the amount of money spent or received under each account. For the check, you write out 4/20/15, Cash, #101, Check from Friend, $500 Debit.

- Debts and credits cancel out. For example, if you spend that $500 on a new oven for your bakery, you would note a $500 debt (Equipment) and a $500 credit (Cash). While you gain $500 in equipment value, you lose $500 in cash.

- Common debits include cash, accounts receivable, equipment, land, wages, and personal funds.
- Common credits include: cash spent, accounts payable, bills, mortgage, and loan payments.
- Remember-- debits are assets and credits are liabilities.

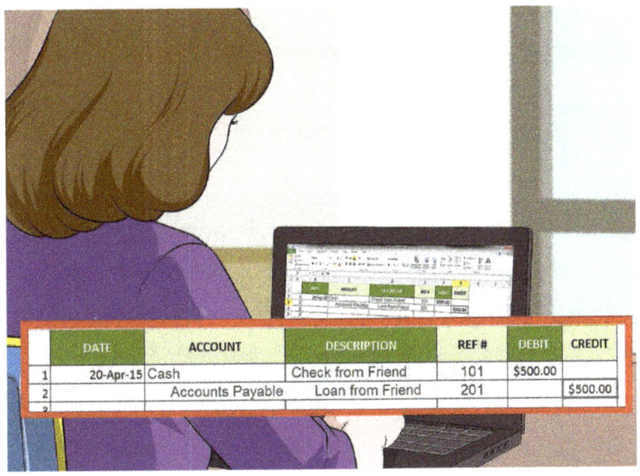

9. Use separate lines for transactions that apply to multiple accounts. For example, that $500 check you received for your business might be a loan, meaning you would have to write it down as both "Cash" and "Accounts Payable. Use separate lines under the same date and description to note both accounts and their amounts.

- 4/20/15, Cash, #101, Check from Friend, $500 Debit
- Accounts Payable, #201, Loan from Friend, $500 Credit

10. Record every single transaction as it happe**ns.** Every time any one of your accounts makes a change, record it in your general journal. Think of this document as the "story" of your finances – it tells the details of every economic interaction your business made in order.

- At the end of the day or week, take all of your receipts and invoices and check them against your journal to make sure you haven't missed anything.

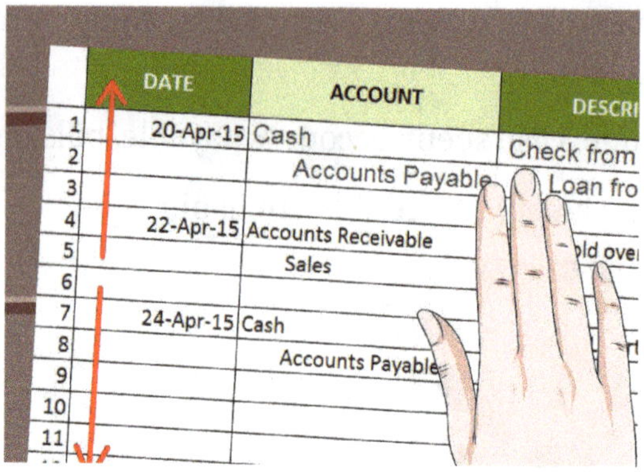

11. Label your journal. Just like you labeled every single account, you should make a label for your journal. An example might be by date, such as "General Journal for 4/1/15 → 5/1/15," or by simply using numbers to place journals chronologically, such as "Journal 1."

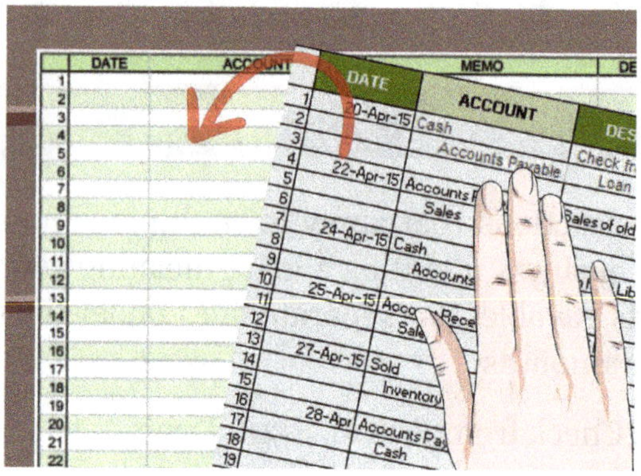

12. Transfer your journal entries to account ledgers regularly. An account ledger notes every transaction by account -- so you have a ledger for Cash, Accounts Receivable, etc. You need to keep both a journal and a ledger so that executives, accountants, and staff can quickly look up your business's financial health by date and by type.

- If possible, make a record in your ledger immediately after writing in the journal.

Part 2. Writing Account Ledgers

1. Use account ledgers to keep track of specific transactions like cash, accounts receivable, or sales.

Journals are where you write the date, details and amount of every single business transaction based on its type. But ledgers break this information up into specific accounts, allowing you to see all of your transactions, like Cash, Accounts Receivable, Sales, on their own sheets.

2. Make a ledger page for each account. Make specific account ledgers based on their name and reference numbers. Your first ledger might be "Cash, #101." This ledger will illustrate every single cash transaction you've made. You will copy your journal entries into the appropriate ledgers, so you need a ledger for every account listed in your journal.

- Consider making a "Chart of Accounts" table of contents page to help you keep track of each account number.
- If you have odd expenses, consider a "general ledger" as well, which collects atypical transactions like tax returns, sales gone bad, personal expenses, etc.

3. Make columns on the far left of the page for the date, journal number, and description. These can be copied directly from your journal entry on the transaction. For the $500 check, you can list "4/20/15, Journal 1, Check from Friend."

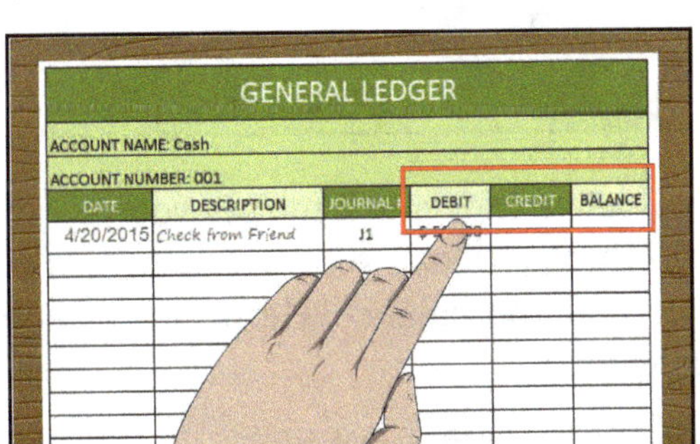

4. Split the rest of the ledger into three sections: Debit, Credit, and Balance. This allows you to

quickly see what you own (debit), what you spend (credit), and how much you still owe (balance.) Your final sheet should look something like this:

Date | Reference | Description | Debit | Credit | Balance |

In a ledger, just like in a journal:

- Debit refers to money you receive.
- Credit refers to money you owe or paid.
- Balance refers to the what you still owe, or the difference between debit and credit.

5. Place any related credits and debits side by side. For example, if you have a $500 loan from a friend, start by noting down $500 as a debit. Say you make your first sale for $200 the next day and decide to start paying your friend back. Mark a new date, 4/21/15, and write $200 under your credit section.

6. Use the balance section to calculate how much money you've earned or still owe. With the last example, you paid back $200 of the $500 loan your friend gave you. Subtract the payment you've made from the total you owe to find you balance. Here, you still owe $300, so note that as your balance to the right of your payment.

- In other words, the Balance = Credit – Debit.
- Not every expense will have a balance. If, for example, you receive a $20,000 research

grant that you don't have to pay back, you just note the $20,000 in the debit column and move on.

7. Remember to make related entries in every account. Returning to the $500 loan from a friend, you must also note that you owe them the money in "Accounts Payable: /4/20/15 | Journal 1 | Loan from Friend | $0 Debit | $500 Credit | $500 Balance. | This must occur every time there is a change to the account. If you decide to pay your friend back, for example, you would need to make a new entry /4/21/15 | Journal 1 | Loan from Friend | $200 Debit | $500 Credit | $300 Remaining |

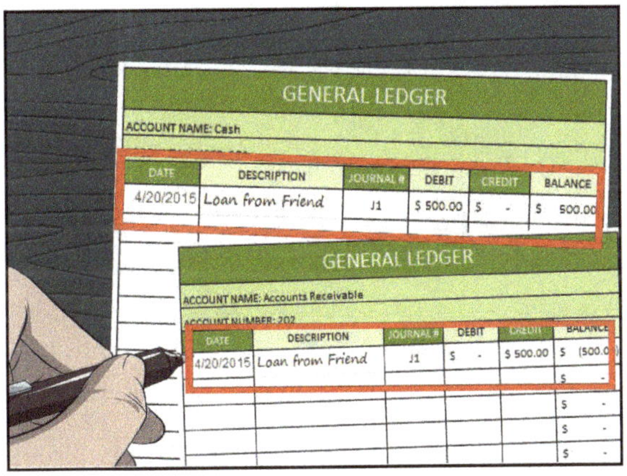

8. Record transactions as they occur. Any time a journal entry is made, that entry should be immediately posted to the ledger. For our example, we have the journal entry: Loan from a friend for $500. This journal entry affects 2 accounts (Cash and Accounts Receivable), so you must make entries to both of those ledger accounts.

- Turn to the Cash page of your ledger. In the left column (which is used for recording debits), write the date of the transaction, and then write the amount. In this example, the amount is $500.
- Turn to the Accounts Receivable page of your ledger. Write the date in the right column (which is used for credits), followed by the transaction amount. In this example, the amount is $500.
- Update these pages as new journal entries arise.

9. Add a "notes" section to help track new information. For example, once you've paid off your total loan of $500, you might write out "Paid in Full" under the description, or a small notes section next to "Balance."

10. Combine different accounts into one book to build your general ledger. A full ledger details every single account so that anyone can flip through it to see exactly how much money is being made/spent in each category. The front page includes the chart of accounts, listing each account in the ledger and its number, such as "Cash, #101," so that people can easily find the information they need.

- Add the accounts to the ledger in order for easy access.

11. Add up the debits and credits at the bottom of the page for each account. This lets you know the total amount you own or owe for each account. If the credits are higher than the debits, then that

account is in losing money. This however, is to be expected – accounts payable will always be in debt, because it is a list of all the money you owe.

12. Add together your total debits and credits and make sure they match. Debit will always equal credit. This is an ironclad rule of accounting, and it makes sense: all of your money had to come from somewhere. If you bought something, you paid for it (credit) and now own it's worth (debt). If there is any discrepancy, check your journal against your ledgers to find anything you forgot to record.

- Remember – any transaction, positive or negative, needs to go into the journal and ledgers.
- Some beginner accountants often forget the idea of "ownership." For example, if you spend $10,000 on the business, then the business technically "owes" you $10,000. If the business was ever sold, you would be paid back your $10,000.

13. Review how to craft a balance sheet if you are struggling to account for all your debts and credits. Balance sheets are snapshots of your business's assets and liabilities. This helpful form lists everything your company owns and owes at any given time, which can help you see any holes in your ledger.

14. Familiarize yourself with the accounting cycle to learn what comes next. Posting to the general

ledger is step 2 in what is known as the accounting cycle. On its own, the ledger wouldn't be very helpful, but used as a part of the cycle, it is an invaluable tool. The accounting cycle can be broken down into a few simplified steps.

- Collect the source documents, like receipts or invoices, that need to be logged.
- Record the transaction in the journal in chronological order.
- Post the journal entries to the ledger accounts.
- Prepare the trial balance. This is a listing of all the ledger accounts pooled together, and it should be prepared at the end of the accounting period.
- Prepare the financial statements. These can be compiled after adjusting the trial balance properly.

How to Reconcile a General Ledger Account

Method 1. Ensuring General Ledger Accuracy

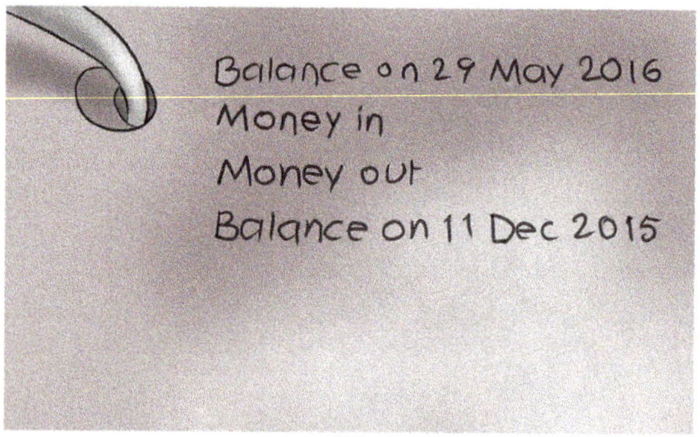

1. Find and compile relevant documents. In addition to the general ledger itself, you will need all of the documents tied to each transaction in the ledger. These include relevant invoices, receipts, account statements, and any other records relating to transactions or expenses. Basically, anything that was used as a source for data for the general ledger for this accounting period must be located and assembled to be readily accessible.

2. Check the beginning account balance. Start by choosing an account within the general ledger to reconcile first. This can be any of the businesses many accounts, from accounts receivable to

inventory to interest expense. It doesn't matter where you start because you'll have to do every account eventually. When you've chosen an account, first make sure that the starting balance for the period recorded in the general ledger matches the ending balance for the same account from the last period. This ensures that any errors detected lie in this period and not in previous periods.

- For example, if you chose the cash account, you would need to make sure that the ending cash balance from the last period was the same as the starting cash balance this period. Any discrepancy would mean that the cash balance was improperly reported at some point and that the business's true current amount of cash is unknown.

3. Match each general ledger entry with its underlying transaction. Go back and look at each transaction that affected this account. If proper accounting procedures were followed, each general ledger entry should have a reference to an invoice or receipt number that will make finding the documents simple. When you've found the documents, make sure that the transactions were recorded just once in each account, for the correct amount, and in the right accounts. Adjust any incorrect amounts and recalculate the total account balances accordingly.

- For example, in the cash account, you would make sure to check transactions where any cash was received from customers or where the company paid out cash.

4. Make sure adjustments and reversals were made properly. Adjustments, which are usually used to comply with accrual accounting standards, and reversals, which change entries made in the previous period, can both cause accounts be imbalanced if they are not implemented properly.

- With adjustments, it is important to check that they were recorded under the right circumstances, for example that an adjustment accounting for services billed but not earned was actually necessary under the circumstances.

- For reversals, also called reversing entries, the important thing to look for is that planned reversals for the period were actually made at the right time. In other words, make sure that anything planned to be reversed was actually reversed.

5. Investigate unusual transactions. To the experience eye, some transactions will stand out as immediately unusual. These transactions are generally those that make balance adjustments that are usually not made. For example, a decrease to a revenue account is usually not made over the course of a regular accounting period. Keep an eye out for any of these unusual transactions and subject any you find to a high level of scrutiny.

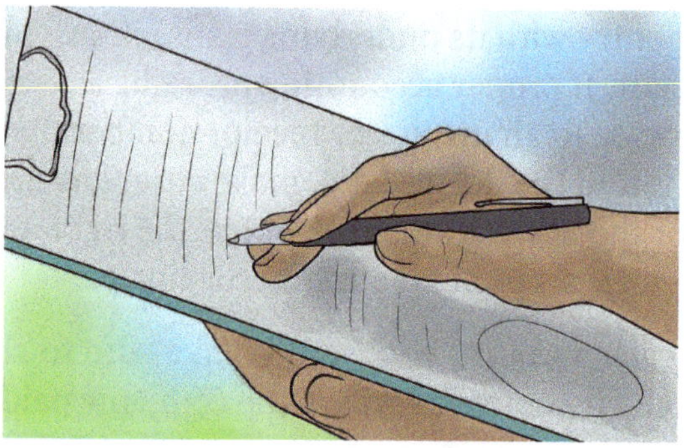

6. Verify the ending balance of the account. After any adjustments for misreported transactions, adjustments, or reversals, check and be sure that the sum of the transactions matches the ending account balance. If your calculated balance doesn't match the actual balance in the account, you have miscalculated something.

7. Repeat for other accounts. Use this same process again to reconcile the other accounts in the general ledger. When you've done so, you will have a completed and reconcile general ledger.

Method 2. Checking Financial Statements

1. Gather the current financial statements. Reconciliation in some cases can also mean making sure that the general ledger balances match the balances reported for the same accounts in that period's financial statements. Start by getting copies of the business's financial statements. You'll need to compare line items on these documents to their equivalent accounts in the general ledger.

2. Investigate revenue and expenses account balance for the income statement. Start by checking to see that the revenue, or sales, account is the same on both the income statement and in the general ledger. If this number doesn't match, almost everything else will be incorrect. If you detect a discrepancy, you'll have to go back and review the revenue account in the general ledger again.

- Next, look at other revenue accounts, like interest income or non-operating income, if applicable. Check these balances against their reported values on the income statement.
- When you've taken care of income values, move on to expense accounts, aggregating expenses into their categories on the income statement where necessary. For example, costs of goods sold would include both the cost of materials for items produced and the direct labor cost incurred.

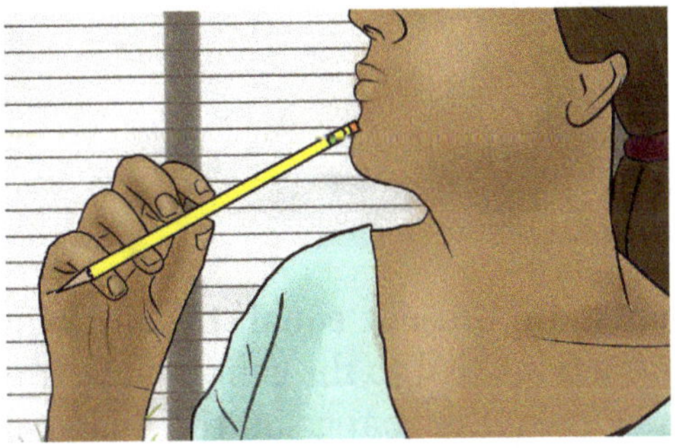

3. Check asset and liability account balances on the balance sheet. Look at the reported asset amounts on the balance sheet, including cash amounts, inventory, fixed assets, and other asset

categories. Make sure that these balance match those reported in the ending account balances in the general ledger. Some of these accounts are aggregated on the balance sheet. For example, cash and cash equivalents can include a number of different types of assets, from actual cash to savings and checking account balances.

- After checking assets, move on to liabilities, looking at the reported short and long term liabilities on the balance sheet. Make sure these match the ending balances recorded in the general ledger.

4. Check balances in the other financial statements. The other financial statements will depend largely on the balances recorded in the first two statements. Make sure to mark if any discrepancies were noticed in the income statement or balance sheet and where any changes to these account might affect the statement of cash flows or shareholder's equity.

5. Make adjustments if accounts still are not equal. If you notice discrepancies, go back and investigate the underlying transactions tied to the general ledger entries. Prove the account balance to be correct first and then make the change on the financial statement. Then, update the other balances affected by this change if your accounting software or spreadsheet doesn't do this for you.

Method 3. Correcting an Unbalanced General Ledger

1. Construct a trial balance. Sometimes, a general ledger can have a final balance that is unevenly split between credits and debits. Ideally, this balance should be zero, as the credit value should match the debit value. If this is not the case, one or a number of transactions have been recorded improperly. To see if there is such a problem, create a trial balance by adding up all of the credits and debits recorded in each account. This calculated balance is called a trial balance.

- Before going further, recheck your math adding the credit and debit columns together. If it is still unbalanced, make sure that you didn't place any values in the wrong column.

2. Investigate credit to debit balances in each account. Compare the balances for each account to the transactions that make up that account. If you find an error, go through again and recalculate the account balance using the credit or debit values from each transaction.

- Follow each transaction to the other account that it effects and make sure an equivalent value for credit was reported for each debit to the original account and vice versa.

3. Correct imbalances in each account, if they still exist. If working from the transactions still fails to balance the accounts, you may have an error in transaction reporting. In this case, you will need

to go back to the source material (receipts, invoices, etc.) to locate the source of the imbalance. Check that the transaction in the source material was recorded correctly in every account that it affects. For example, for a customer purchase with cash, check that equivalent entries were made in cash, sales, inventory, and cost of goods sold and that these entries balance to zero.

4. Verify that the trial balance is now zero. After locating all errors you can find and adjusting them to their correct places and values, run another trial balance calculation to make sure that you've fixed the problem. If you haven't, go back and repeat the process, checking back over your work from the first time.

How to Understand Debits and Credits

In bookkeeping under General Accepted Accounting Principles (GAAP), debits and credits are used to track the changes of account values. They can also be thought of as mirror opposites: Each debit to an account must be accompanied by a credit to another account (that's how the phrase "double-entry bookkeeping" gets its name). Understanding debits and credits is essential for bookkeeping and analysis of balance sheets.

Steps

Part 1. Learning the Terms

1. Familiarize yourself with the meaning of "debit" and "credit." In bookkeeping, the words "debit" and "credit" have very distinct meanings and a close relationship. Debits and credits balance

each other out —if a debit is added to one account, then a credit must be added to the an opposite account.

- In accounting, the debit column is on the left of an accounting entry, while credits are on the right.
- Debits increase asset or expense accounts and decrease liability or equity. Credits do the opposite — decrease assets and expenses and increase liability and equity.
- To make sense of this, take a look at the basic accounting equation, which is Assets = Equity + Liabilities. Assets are paid for by equity and/or liability —you cannot have one without the other. So if you complete a transaction that increases assets (and you debit the asset account), you must also increase the equity or liability (by crediting the equity or liability account) so that Assets remain equal to Equity and/or Liability.

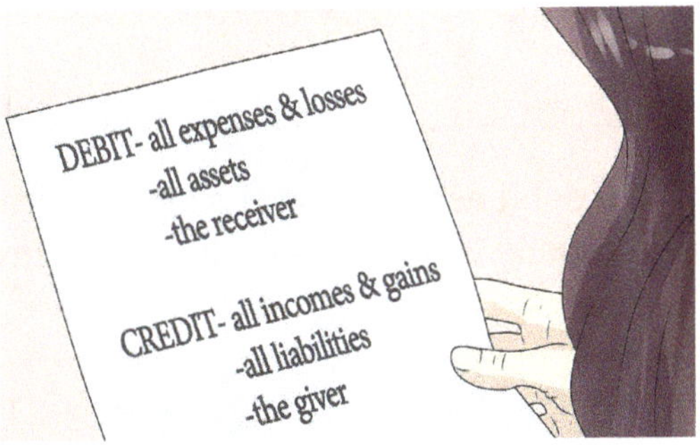

2. Use acronyms to remember the difference. One of the simplest ways to remember the difference between a debit and a credit is with the use of familiar acronyms.

- Generally, these types of accounts are increased with a debit: Dividends, Expenses, Assets, Losses (DEAL).
- Generally, these types of accounts are increased with a credit: Gains, Income, Revenues, Liabilities, Stockholders' Equity (GIRLS).

3. Remember that the books must be kept in balance. Remember that if you debit one account, you're going to need to credit the opposite account. Whenever there is an accounting transaction, at least two accounts will always be impacted. The total amount of debits in a single transaction must equal the total amount of credits.

- For example, if you pay down your Accounts Payable account (a liability) with $20,000 in cash (an asset), you'll need to adjust both accounts.

- In that case, you'll credit Cash for $20,000. That will reduce your cash amount by $20,000.
- To keep your books in balance, you'll need to debit Accounts Payable by $20,000. That will likewise reduce your Accounts Payable amount by $20,000.

Part 2. Recording Debits and Credits Correctly

1. Set up the balance sheet with all debit accounts on the left and credit accounts on the right. For illustration, assume that ABC Company has $5000 cash, $7000 inventory, $3000 capital stock, and $9000 surplus.

2. Set up the ledgers for each account. A general ledger is a standard way of recording debits and credits for a particular account.

- Place the debit balance on the left and the credit balance on the right. Remember that debit accounts have debit balances and credit accounts have credit balances.

3. Consider what is being exchanged when entering a transaction. Whenever a transaction occurs, something is being exchanged for something else. For example: Does the transaction change the

amount of cash, the amount of receivables, the inventory value, or add to an expense? Suppose the company in our example has subsequently sold on credit $4,000, which cost it $2,800, and incurred various expenses totaling $500 paid in cash. So this transaction impacted the following accounts: Accounts Receivables, Inventory, Cash, and Surplus (for simplicity, all all profit and loss as credit or debit will be logged in the Surplus account).

- If the transaction increases a debit account, record a debit entry in that debit account, and simultaneously a credit entry in an appropriate credit account.
- Continuing with our example, you would debit Accounts Receivables $4,000, then credit Surplus with a corresponding $4,000.
- If the transaction decreases a debit account, record a credit entry in that debit account, and simultaneously a debit entry in an appropriate credit account.
- The cost of goods sold of $2,800 decreases the inventory, and is therefore a credit entry. It will have a corresponding $2,800 debit entry from Surplus. The $500 expenses paid in cash decreases the debit account Cash, so you would enter $500 credit in the Cash account. It will have a corresponding $500 debit entry from Surplus.

4. Calculate the ending balance in each account and update the balance sheet. Remember, your balance sheet is appropriately named because it must always stay in balance. The overall value of your assets must equal the value of your liabilities plus the value of your equity.

How to Understand and Set up a General Ledger

Steps

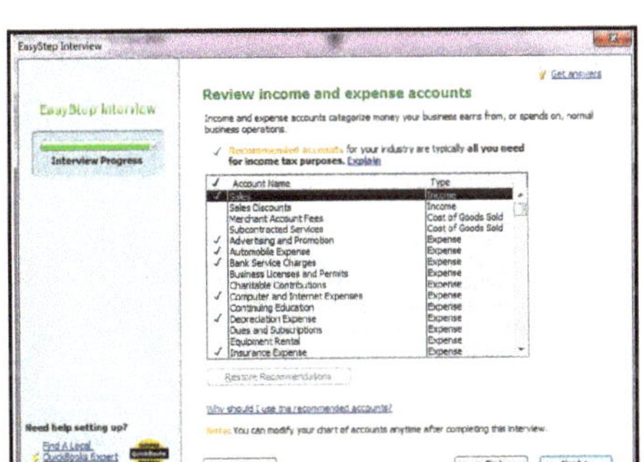

1. Establish the type of chart of accounts you wish to use. This may be one of the sample charts

provided with your software, or you may wish to modify an existing chart or enter a new chart from scratch. If you are not qualified to decide the best approach consult with your accountant. Remember that you can always add more chart of account codes in the future. Later on you can also remove chart codes that you have never used. In other words, the structure of the chart need not be absolutely final, but the overall structure should be in place.

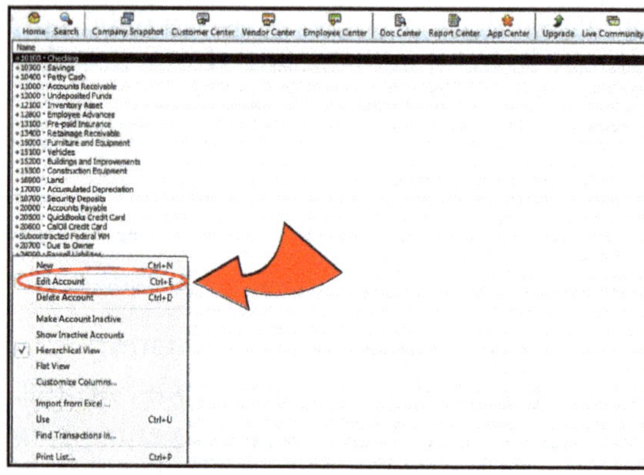

2. Once you have established the chart of accounts, edit or delete any existing chart codes and enter your new chart codes if required.

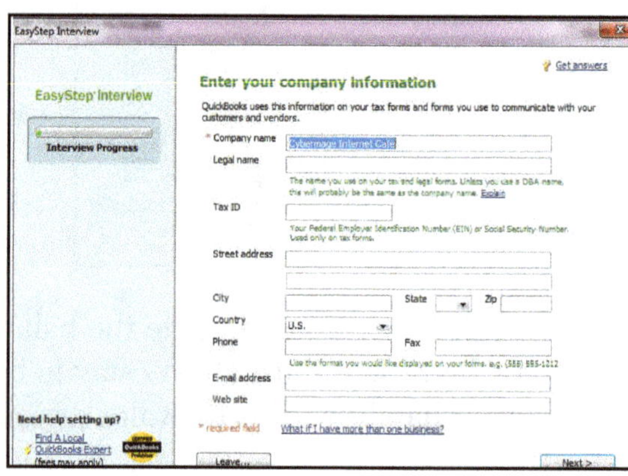

3. Enter your company details into the program, and enter the account code for any 'special' accounts such as your retained earnings account, suspense account and other accounts if required.

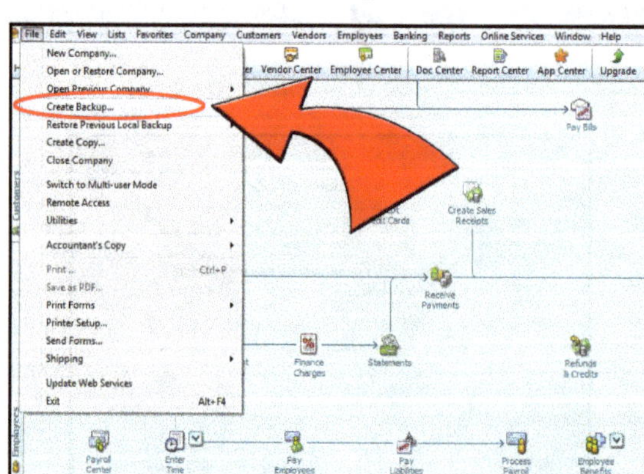

4. Make a back-up. Keep this for future reference.

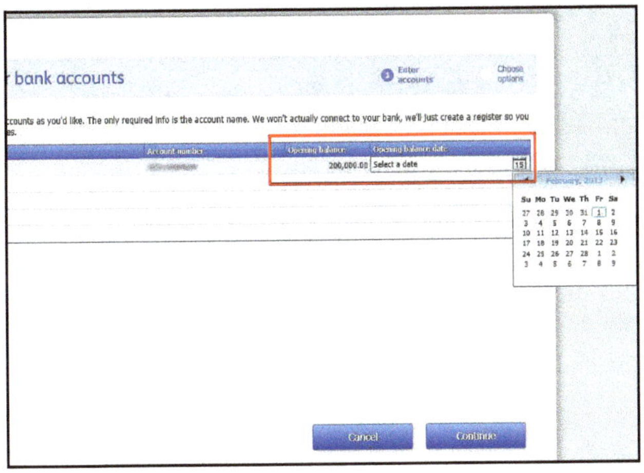

5. Enter your opening balances for the year. Establish whether you will be entering balances starting from period 1 (recommended) or if you will be entering balances from the prior period only. If you will be entering balances from the previous period only, you will require a trial balance report from which to work, up to the previous period.

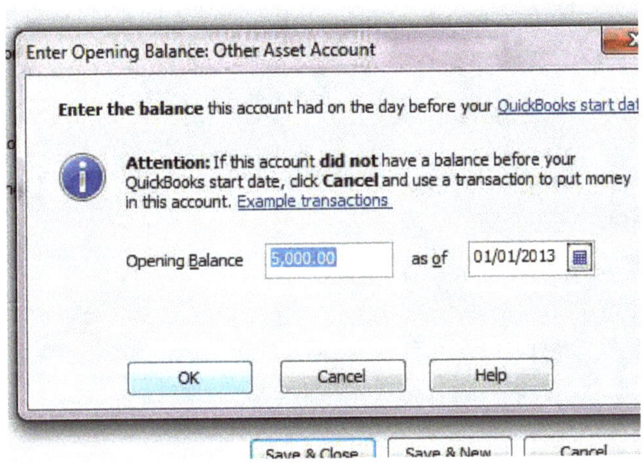

6. Enter and if necessary post your opening balances.

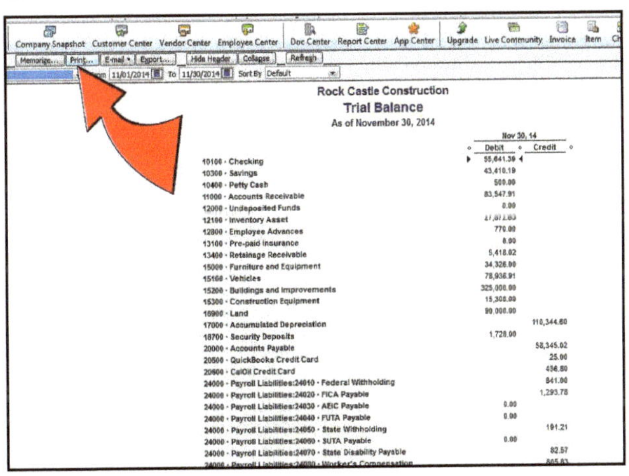

7. Print a trial balance and check it.

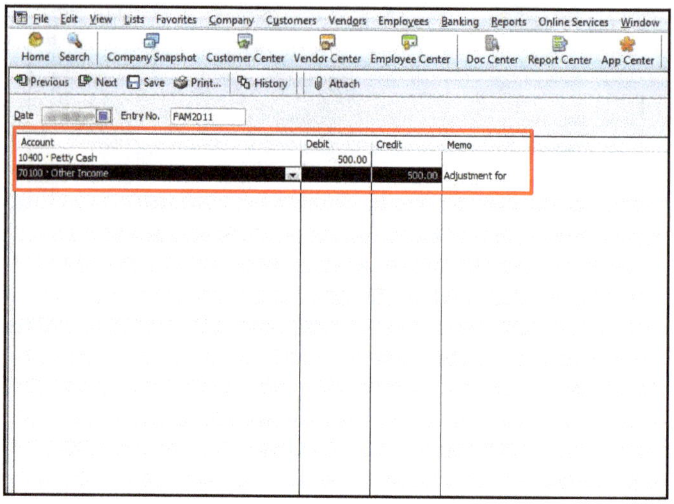

8. If necessary, enter any correcting balances.

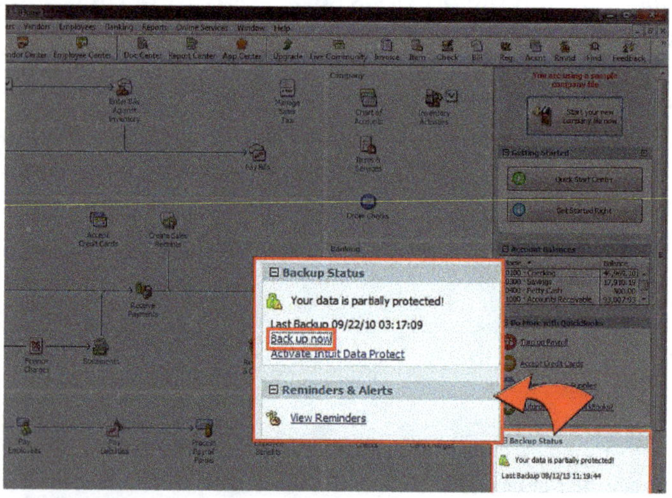

9. Make a backup at this stage for future reference.

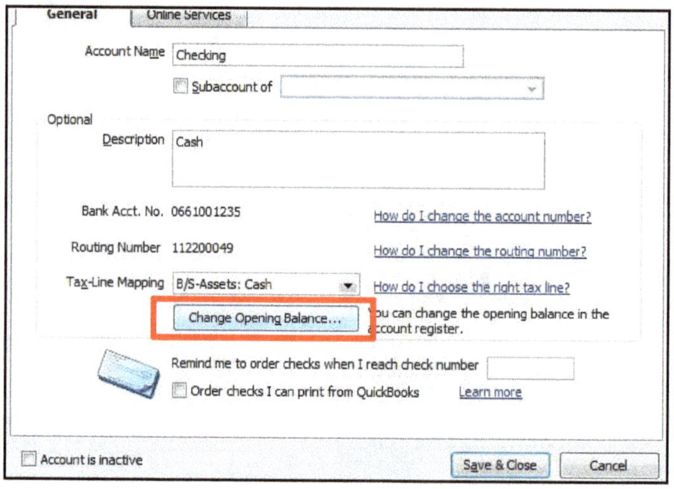

10. Optionally enter your last year balances if your software allows you to.

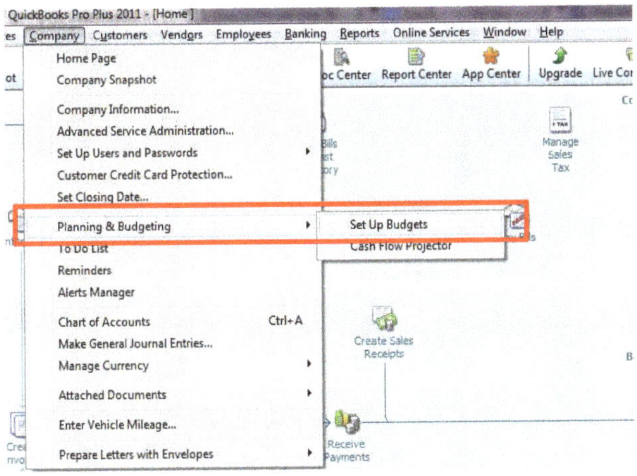

11. Optionally enter your budgets if you wish to print reports that compare actuals to budgets and your software allows you to.

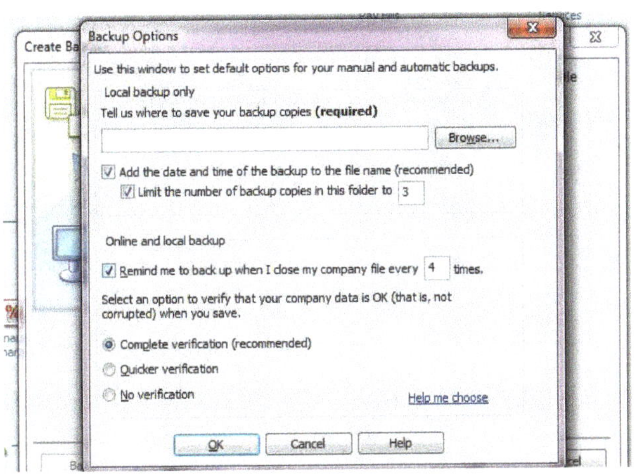

12. Make a backup at this stage for future reference.

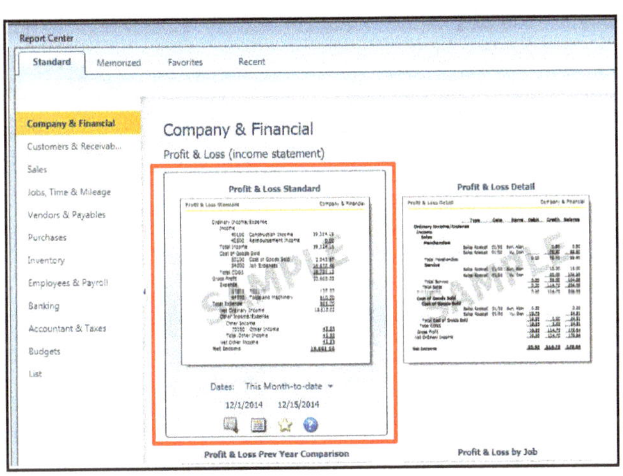

13. Carefully check your financial statements. Make sure the columns add up correctly and that the internal calculations on your reports are correct. This is a critical point. Do not assume your reports are correct if you have modified your chart of accounts structure.

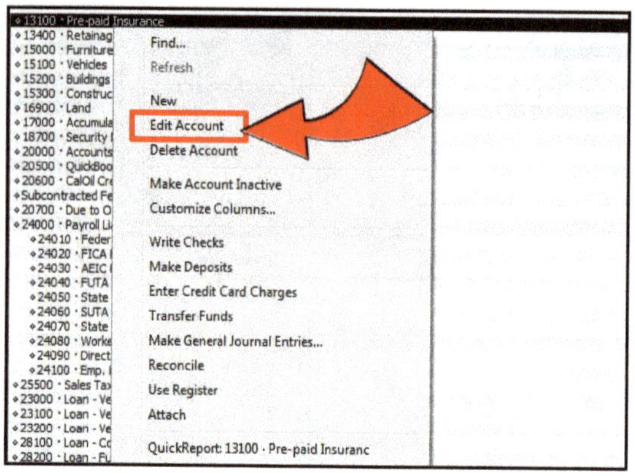

14. If the financial reports are not correct, edit/correct them. Do this by moving account codes to their correct locations if possible.

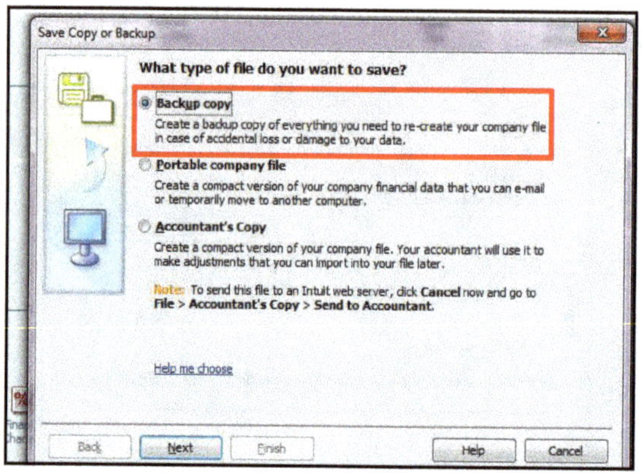

15. Make one final backup. Your system should now be ready for general use.

Double-entry Bookkeeping

All businesses, whether they use the cash-basis accounting method or the accrual accounting method, use double-entry bookkeeping to keep their books. Double-entry accounting is a practice that helps minimize errors and increases the chance that your books balance. This method gets its name because you enter all transactions twice.

When it comes to double-entry bookkeeping, the key formula for the balance sheet (Assets = Liabilities + Equity) plays a major role.

In order to adjust the balance of accounts in the bookkeeping world, you use a combination of debits and credits. You may think of a debit as a subtraction because you've found that debits usually mean a decrease in your bank balance. And, you've probably found unexpected credits in your bank or credit card account that mean more money has been added in your favor. Now forget what you've learned about debits or credits. In bookkeeping, their meanings aren't so simple.

The only definite thing when it comes to debits and credits in the bookkeeping world is that a debit is on the left side of a transaction and a credit is on the right side of a transaction.

Double-entry Bookkeeping Example: Purchasing an Item with Cash

Here's an example of the practice in action. Suppose you purchase a new desk that costs $1,500 for your office. This transaction actually has two parts: You spend an asset — cash — to buy another asset — furniture. So, you must adjust two accounts in your company's books: the Cash account and the Furniture account. Here's what the transaction looks like in a bookkeeping entry:

Double-Entry Bookkeeping: Purchasing an Item with Cash		
Account	Debit	Credit
Furniture	$1,500	
Cash		$1,500

In this transaction, you record the accounts impacted by the transaction. The debit increases the value of the Furniture account, and the credit decreases the value of the Cash account. For this transaction, both accounts impacted are asset accounts, so, looking at how the balance sheet is affected, you can see that the only changes are to the asset side of the balance sheet equation:

Assets = Liabilities + Equity

Furniture increase = No change to this side of the equation

Cash decrease

In this case, the books stay in balance because the exact dollar amount that increases the value of your Furniture account decreases the value of your Cash account. At the bottom of any journal entry, you should include a brief description that explains the purpose for the entry.

Double-entry Accounting Example: Purchasing Items on Credit

To show you how you record a transaction if it impacts both sides of the balance sheet equation, here's an example that shows how to record the purchase of inventory. Suppose that you purchase $5,000 worth of widgets on credit.

These new widgets add value to your Inventory Asset account and they also add to your Accounts Payable account. (Remember, the Accounts Payable account is a Liability account where you track bills that need to be paid at some point in the future.) Here's how the double-entry bookkeeping transaction for your widget purchase looks:

Double-Entry Accounting Example: Purchasing Items on Credit		
Account	Debit	Credit
Inventory	$5,000	
Accounts Payable		$5,000

Here's how this transaction affects the balance sheet equation:

Assets = Liabilities + Equity

Inventory increases = Accounts Payable increases + No change

In this case, the books stay in balance because both sides of the equation increase by $5,000.

You can see from the two example transactions how double-entry accounting helps to keep your books in balance — as long as you make sure each entry into the books is balanced. Balancing your entries may look simple here, but sometimes bookkeeping entries can get very complex when more than two accounts are impacted by the transaction.

How to do Double Entry Bookkeeping

Step 1: Identify and Analyze Transactions

The accounting cycle starts by identifying the transactions which relate to the business. The business is a separate entity to the owner, so only business transactions should be included.

Having identified the transactions, each one now needs to be analyzed to determine which accounts in the bookkeeping records are affected. Each transaction must be supported by a relevant accounting source document such as sales and purchases invoices, debit and credit notes, petty cash vouchers, payroll reports etc.

Step 2: Journal Entries for Transactions

The journal entries are recorded in a journal sometimes referred to as a daybook.

Step 3: Post Journals to Ledgers

The journals are used to post to the subsidiary and general ledgers (sometimes referred to as the book of final entry). The general ledger has an account for each type of transaction e.g. rent expense, accounts receivable control, fixed assets etc. The general ledger is sometimes divided into the nominal ledger for income and expenses, and the private ledger for assets and liabilities.

All postings to the ledgers are double entry postings and therefore must balance which every debit having an equal and opposite credit entry.

Step 4: Prepare an Unadjusted Trial Balance

At the end of each accounting period, the balances on the accounts of the general ledger are listed to produce a trial balance. At this stage the total debits on the trial balance should equal the total credits.

This unadjusted trial balance is used solely to check the total of the debit and credit entries, to ensure the accounting records balance. If the trial balance does not balance correcting entries should be made in the ledgers until it does.

Step 5: Prepare Worksheet

A 10 column worksheet is prepared and the unadjusted trial balance is transferred to the first two columns.

Step 6: Record Adjusting Journal Entries

Adjusting entries such as accruals, prepayments, and depreciation entries are prepared to ensure that income and expenditure is allocated to the correct accounting period, this means that the accounting records are completed on an accruals basis and are in compliance with the matching principle.The adjusting entries are entered in the next two columns of the worksheet and at this stage, are not entered into the accounting records.

Step 7: Adjusted trial balance

When all adjusting entries have been completed an adjusted trial balance is prepared in the next two columns of the worksheet.

Step 8: Prepare Financial Statements

The financial statements can now be prepared from the adjusted trial balance. Items relating to the income statement are transferred to the next two columns and items relating to the balance sheet are transferred to the final two columns.

Step 9: Closing Entries

Closing entries are carried out in the accounting ledgers. Closing entries are posted and temporary income and expenditure accounts are closed and their balances transferred to an income and expenditure summary account.

The summary account is in turn closed to transfer the profit or loss for the period to the balance sheet retained profits account. Balance sheet or permanent accounts are not closed, but the balance is carried forward to the next accounting period.

Step 10: Post Closing Trial Balance

A post closing trial balance is drawn up to ensure that the debits and credits balance for the start of the new accounting period.

The post closing trial balance is a list of balances after the closing entries have been made. At this stage the temporary income and expenditure accounts have been closed and set to zero, so only the balance sheet accounts are listed on the post closing trial balance. The accounting cycle starts again with the new opening balance sheet account balances.

How to Write a Financial Statement

Financial statements are the formal record of a company's financial activity. The main components of a financial statement are the balance sheet, the income statement, and the statement of cash flows. The balance sheet shows the assets, liabilities, and the shareholder's equity at a specific point in time. The income sheet, on the other hand, shows the revenues, expenses, and income or loss for specific period of time, usually a month, quarter, or year. The statement of cash flows shows the cash balance at the beginning of a period, the inflows and outflows of cash during a specific period, and the ending cash balance. For public companies, what goes on these sheets is regulated by the Securities

Exchange Commission in compliance with Generally Accepted Accounting Principles (GAAP) established by the Financial Accounting Standards Board (FASB). You should hire a professional to make sure you are compliant with those standards if you are unfamiliar with them.

Part 1. Building a Balance Sheet

1. Understand the basics of the balance sheet. The balance sheet is called so because it shows the company's balance between assets and liabilities. The key underlying basis of the balance sheet is the basic accounting equation, which is Total Assets=Liabilities+Shareholder's. Rearranging the equation, you can see that equity is equal to assets minus liabilities. The balance sheet reflects this relationship. All assets and liabilities are listed and added up on the balance sheet, then liabilities are subtracted from assets to arrive at a figure for shareholder's equity.

- Balance sheets may be constructed using accounting software. Or, you can simply create a spreadsheet or written list with two columns that can be used to total your assets and liabilities by category.

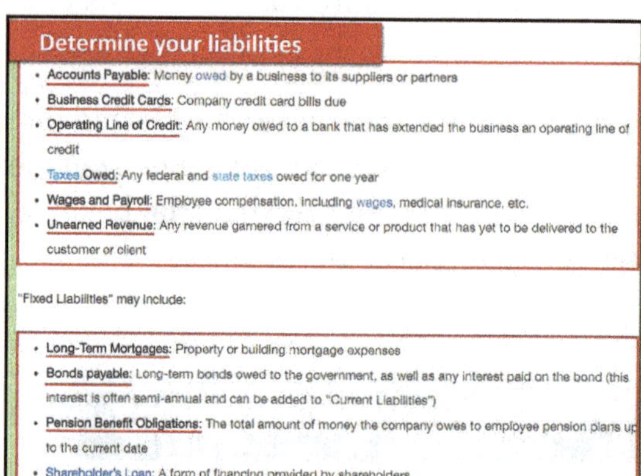

Determine your liabilities

- Accounts Payable: Money owed by a business to its suppliers or partners
- Business Credit Cards: Company credit card bills due
- Operating Line of Credit: Any money owed to a bank that has extended the business an operating line of credit
- Taxes Owed: Any federal and state taxes owed for one year
- Wages and Payroll: Employee compensation, including wages, medical insurance, etc.
- Unearned Revenue: Any revenue garnered from a service or product that has yet to be delivered to the customer or client

"Fixed Liabilities" may include:

- Long-Term Mortgages: Property or building mortgage expenses
- Bonds payable: Long-term bonds owed to the government, as well as any interest paid on the bond (this interest is often semi-annual and can be added to "Current Liabilities")
- Pension Benefit Obligations: The total amount of money the company owes to employee pension plans up to the current date
- Shareholder's Loan: A form of financing provided by shareholders

2. Determine your liabilities. Your liabilities are what the company owes or has paid to other companies or people, including employees. In other words, it's the company's debt. These assets are also divided into "current" and "long-term" categories.

- Current liabilities include things like what you owe on lines of credit and credit cards, as well as anything owed to other companies for goods and supplies. It also includes the income and wages you've paid out to employees and taxes owed, along with unpaid rent and utilities.

- Long-term liabilities include long-term loans payable, bonds payable, and other liabilities that will be paid out over a time period longer than one year.

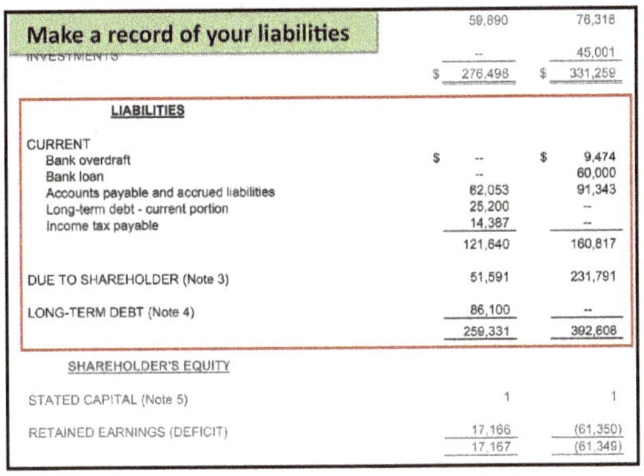

	59,890	76,318
INVESTMENTS	--	45,001
	$ 276,498	$ 331,259
LIABILITIES		
CURRENT		
Bank overdraft	$ --	$ 9,474
Bank loan	--	60,000
Accounts payable and accrued liabilities	82,053	91,343
Long-term debt - current portion	25,200	--
Income tax payable	14,387	--
	121,640	160,817
DUE TO SHAREHOLDER (Note 3)	51,591	231,791
LONG-TERM DEBT (Note 4)	86,100	--
	259,331	392,608
SHAREHOLDER'S EQUITY		
STATED CAPITAL (Note 5)	1	1
RETAINED EARNINGS (DEFICIT)	17,166	(61,350)
	17,167	(61,349)

3. Make a record of your liabilities. Just like your assets, you need to account for each liability (in major categories, such as loans, mortgages, and so on). Also, divide your liabilities on your balance sheet into current and long-term. List liabilities by category and include the value of each category next to the its name. Add up all your liabilities to get your total.

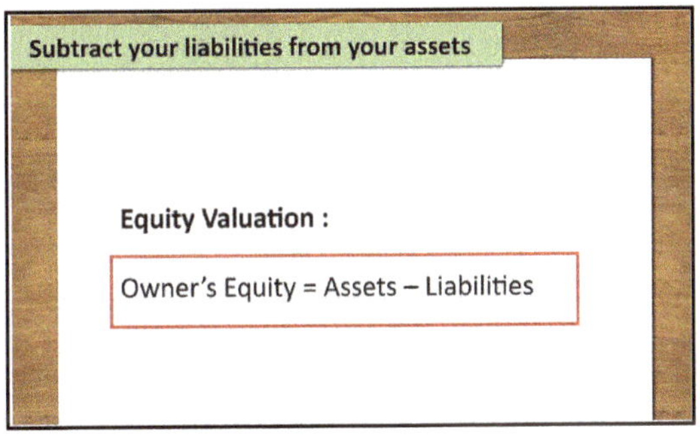

4. Subtract your liabilities from your assets. To figure out the shareholder's equity (also called shareholder's equity), you subtract what is owed from what assets you have. A positive amount of equity indicates that the company has financed its operations with its own money or that of investors, rather than relying as strongly on debt.

   - Have a line for your total assets. Below it, have a line for your total liabilities. Show what the shareholder's equity is when you subtract the second from the first.

5. Expand on shareholder's equity. On your sheet, have a section where you show what the

shareholder's equity is. This section will include items that represent the shareholder's interests in the company. For example, common stock, preferred stock, capital in excess of par, and retained earnings are all common shareholder's equity categories.

- When you've listed these categories out, sum them up to arrive at total shareholder's equity.
- Compare your total to the difference between assets and liabilities from your earlier calculations. If the figures don't match, either you or the accountant that keeps the company's books has made a mistake somewhere along the way.
- Many balance sheets are organized such that the assets are totaled on the left and liabilities and shareholder's equity are totaled on the right. This provides a more literal representation of the basic accounting equation.

Part 2. Writing the Income Statement

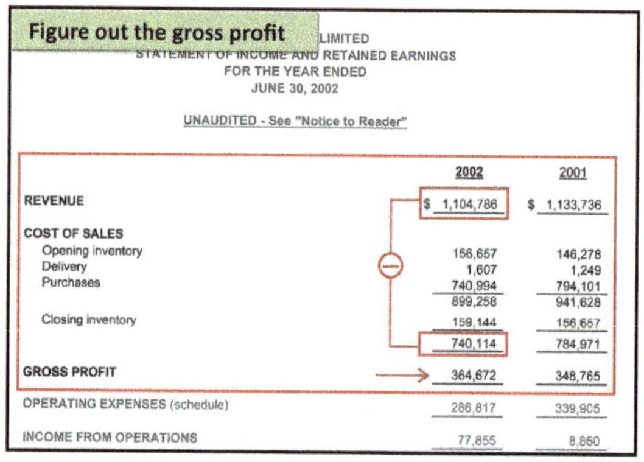
Figure out the gross profit

LIMITED
STATEMENT OF INCOME AND RETAINED EARNINGS
FOR THE YEAR ENDED
JUNE 30, 2002

UNAUDITED - See "Notice to Reader"

	2002	2001
REVENUE	$ 1,104,786	$ 1,133,736
COST OF SALES		
Opening inventory	156,657	146,278
Delivery	1,607	1,249
Purchases	740,994	794,101
	899,258	941,628
Closing inventory	159,144	156,657
	740,114	784,971
GROSS PROFIT	364,672	348,765
OPERATING EXPENSES (schedule)	286,817	339,905
INCOME FROM OPERATIONS	77,855	8,860

1. Start with net sales. As a general rule, the first figure listed in the a company's balance sheet is net sales for the period in question. The income statement may just say "sales" or "revenue," but the figure used is net sales. Net sales represents the gross sales (total sales in the period) minus any returns, discounts, or allowance for lost or damaged goods. This is the company's "top line" and is the truest representation of sales over the period.

- Unlike the balance sheet, the income statement covers financial activity throughout the period in question, whether that is a month, a quarter, or a year.
- The income statement is organized as a reduction of net sales by various expenses faced by the company to arrive at net income (also called net profit or the bottom line).

2. Calculate gross profit. Your first calculation on the income statement will be that for gross profit.

Gross profit represents the company's profit after considering the cost of goods sold (or services provided/sales). Cost of goods sold includes the cost of all materials and labor that went directly towards producing the products that were sold over the period. Total this amount and subtract it from net sales to arrive at gross profit.

3. List the company's operating expenses. On the balance sheet, expenses are separated into two major categories: operating and non-operating expenses. Operating expenses follow the same philosophy as cost of goods sold. That is, they are those expenses related directly to the operations of the company. This includes the cost of selling and advertising products, administrative costs, and wages for employees involved in these departments. It also includes general expenses, such as utilities, rent, and manager salaries.Remember that materials and manufacturing labor costs were already covered in the cost of goods sold and do not need to be counted here.

- Separate these expenses into three major categories: selling, general and administrative expenses. When you've written out the amount of each expense, total them to find total operating expenses.
- Subtract total operating expenses from gross profit to arrive at operating income.

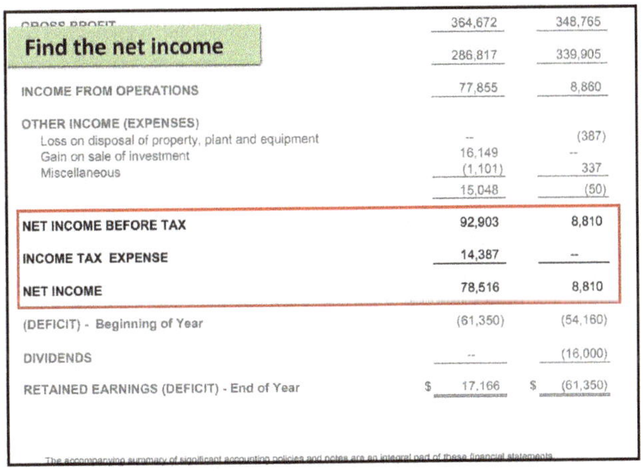

Find the net income

GROSS PROFIT	364,672	348,765
	286,817	339,905
INCOME FROM OPERATIONS	77,855	8,860
OTHER INCOME (EXPENSES)		
Loss on disposal of property, plant and equipment	--	(387)
Gain on sale of investment	16,149	--
Miscellaneous	(1,101)	337
	15,048	(50)
NET INCOME BEFORE TAX	**92,903**	**8,810**
INCOME TAX EXPENSE	**14,387**	**--**
NET INCOME	**78,516**	**8,810**
(DEFICIT) - Beginning of Year	(61,350)	(54,160)
DIVIDENDS	--	(16,000)
RETAINED EARNINGS (DEFICIT) - End of Year	$ 17,166	$ (61,350)

The accompanying summary of significant accounting policies and notes are an integral part of these financial statements

4. Write out non-operating expenses. The other category of expenses on the income statement, non-operating expenses, are those expenses that are not directly related to operations. These include interest, amortization, depreciation, and tax expenses. There is also room in this section

to record an "extraordinary gain or loss," which might arise from a massive amount of inventory theft, for example.

Lay out your income statement

Income Statement For Company XYZ FY 2008 and 2009

(Figures USD)	*2008*	*2009*
Net Sales	1,500,000	2,000,000
Cost of Sales	(350,000)	(375,000)
Gross Income	1,150,000	1,625,000
Operating Expenses (SG&A)	(235,000)	(260,000)
Operating Income	915,000	1,365,000
Other Income (Expense)	40,000	60,000
Extraordinary Gain (Loss)	-	(15,000)
Interest Expense	(50,000)	(50,000)
Net Profit Before Taxes (Pretax Income)	905,000	1,360,000
Taxes	(300,000)	(475,000)
Net Income	605,000	885,000

Now that we understand the anatomy of an income statement, we can deduce from the above

5. Lay out your income statement. As you go, lay out each piece of your income statement. Net sales will be at the top. Each piece will follow in sequential order.

- Put the net sales on one line. Underneath that, put the cost of sales. Below that, subtract the cost of sales from the net sales to get the gross profit. Skip a line before moving on to operating costs.
- Put the operating costs in general categories underneath the gross profit. Generally, selling, general, and administrative costs are lumped into one, but not always. Underneath that, write the operating income that you derived from subtracting the operating costs from the gross profit.
- Next, have a line each for the interest and the taxes. You can subtract them separately or together. Separately gives you more precise data.
- The final line should be the net income.

Part 3. Writing the Statement of Cash Flows

Start with the net income

JUNE 30, 2002

UNAUDITED - See "Notice to Reader"

	2002	2001
CASH FLOWS FROM OPERATING ACTIVITIES		
Net income for the year	$ 78,516	$ 8,810
Adjustment for:		
Amortization	17,854	16,856
Loss on disposal of property, plant and equipment	--	387
Gain on disposal of investment	(16,149)	--
Cash derived from operations	80,221	26,053
Decrease (increase) in working capital items		
Accounts receivable	7,625	23,380
Deposits and prepaid expenses	(254)	688
Inventory	(2,487)	(904)
Accounts payable and accrued liabilities	(9,290)	34,543
Long-term debt - current portion	25,200	--
Income tax payable	14,387	2,206
Cash flows from operating activities	115,402	85,966

1. Start with the net income. The cash flow is an essential number to the company because it establishes the actual cash you have on hand. It's different from your income because your income includes non-cash expenses and assets that do not affect your actual cash balance. However, in

order to create a statement of cash flows, you will first need a completed income statement and completed balance sheets from this period and the previous period.

- The statement of cash flows is split into three pieces: cash flows from operating activities, cash flows from investing activities, and cash flows from financing activities.

Add non-cash expenses back in

	2002	2001
CASH FLOWS FROM OPERATING ACTIVITIES		
Net income for the year	$ 78,516	$ 8,810
Adjustment for:		
Amortization	17,854	16,856
Loss on disposal of property, plant and equipment	--	387
Gain on disposal of investment	(16,149)	--
Cash derived from operations	80,221	26,053
Decrease (increase) in working capital items		
Accounts receivable	7,625	23,380
Deposits and prepaid expenses	(254)	688
Inventory	(2,487)	(904)
Accounts payable and accrued liabilities	(9,290)	34,543
Long-term debt - current portion	25,200	--
Income tax payable	14,387	2,206
Cash flows from operating activities	115,402	85,966
CASH FLOWS FROM INVESTING ACTIVITIES		
Acquisition of property, plant and equipment	(1,426)	(10,342)
Proceeds from disposal of property, plant and equipment	--	3,113
Proceeds from disposal of investment	61,150	--
Dividends	--	(16,000)

2. Begin calculating cash flows from operating activities. With operations, you're looking at how much operations brings in through cash. This step is different from what you did in your other statements because those statements include non-cash items. Here, you are focusing solely on cash. In other words, you must add some things back into the net income because they weren't really cash expenses, and therefore, won't affect the money you have to work with right now. Start with non-cash items, things like amortization and depreciation.

- Amortization is when the company spreads out the cost of something over time for accounting purposes. However, it is not really a cost taking away from cash flow right now. Therefore, you add that expense back in.
- The same with depreciation. It's a number taken away from the total amount of an asset, as it loses value over time. However, it's not technically a cash flow problem, so that expense is added back in.
- This method is the indirect method of figuring out cash flow. The direct method involves adding up cash flows from scratch rather than starting with net income.

Figure out your cash flow in the rest of operations

	2002	2001
Net income for the year	$ 78,516	$ 8,810
Adjustment for:		
Amortization	17,854	16,856
Loss on disposal of property, plant and equipment	--	387
Gain on disposal of investment	(16,149)	--
Cash derived from operations	80,221	26,053
Decrease (increase) in working capital items		
Accounts receivable	7,625	23,380
Deposits and prepaid expenses	(254)	688
Inventory	(2,487)	(904)
Accounts payable and accrued liabilities	(9,290)	34,543
Long-term debt - current portion	25,200	--
Income tax payable	14,387	2,206
Cash flows from operating activities	115,402	85,966
CASH FLOWS FROM INVESTING ACTIVITIES		
Acquisition of property, plant and equipment	(1,426)	(10,342)
Proceeds from disposal of property, plant and equipment	--	3,113
Proceeds from disposal of investment	61,150	--
Dividends	--	(16,000)
Cash flows from investing activities	59,724	(23,229)

3. Figure out your cash flow in the rest of operations. Now you need to look at other items that

bring in or take out cash through operations. For instance, gains or losses on sales of fixed assets are included in this category, as this activity brings in (or draws out) cash.

- If you have sold fixed assets within the period, such as property, you need to look at whether it was a gain or loss, then add or subtract it from the operating costs.
- You also need to look at changes in accounts receivable. Since accounts receivable is what other people owe the company, if it goes down, that means the company has gained cash, and that needs to be added in.
- On the other hand, if the company has bought inventory, that signals a decrease in cash, and needs to be subtracted from the cash flow.
- Other items that can affect the cash flow include taxes payable, insurance you've already paid, and salaries payable.

Determine the cash you have on hand based on investing

Inventory	(2,487)	(904)
Accounts payable and accrued liabilities	(9,290)	34,543
Long-term debt - current portion	25,200	--
Income tax payable	14,387	2,206
Cash flows from operating activities	115,402	85,966
CASH FLOWS FROM INVESTING ACTIVITIES		
Acquisition of property, plant and equipment	(1,426)	(10,342)
Proceeds from disposal of property, plant and equipment	--	3,113
Proceeds from disposal of investment	61,150	--
Dividends	--	(16,000)
Cash flows from investing activities	59,724	(23,229)
CASH FLOWS FROM FINANCING ACTIVITIES		
Advances from (repayments to) shareholder	(180,200)	(150,000)
Acquisition of (repayment of) long-term debt	86,100	--
	(94,100)	(150,000)
NET INCREASE (DECREASE) IN CASH RESOURCES	81,026	(87,263)

4. Determine cash flows from investing activities. Like with operations, you need to examine how investing has affected your overall cash flow. This category is focused on long-term investments, such as equipment and buildings. This category mainly focuses on where cash has gone in the current year when it has been invested.

- This step can include money you've put into new equipment or other capital, such as buildings, which will be subtracted from cash flow. It can also be equipment you've sold, which would be added into the cash flow.
- This step also includes any money invested in the stock market, what you've bought and sold, and how that affects your overall cash.

Look at the cash available from financing

Cash flows from operating activities	115,402	85,966
CASH FLOWS FROM INVESTING ACTIVITIES		
Acquisition of property, plant and equipment	(1,426)	(10,342)
Proceeds from disposal of property, plant and equipment	--	3,113
Proceeds from disposal of investment	61,150	--
Dividends	--	(16,000)
Cash flows from investing activities	59,724	(23,229)
CASH FLOWS FROM FINANCING ACTIVITIES		
Advances from (repayments to) shareholder	(180,200)	(150,000)
Acquisition of (repayment of) long-term debt	86,100	--
	(94,100)	(150,000)
NET INCREASE (DECREASE) IN CASH RESOURCES	81,026	(87,263)
CASH (DEFICIENCY) RESOURCES - Beginning of Year	(69,474)	17,789
CASH RESOURCES (DEFICIENCY) - End of Year	$ 11,552	$ (69,474)
Cash resources (deficiency) is comprised of:		
Cash	$ 11,552	$ --

5. Look at the cash available from financing. The third category is financing. This section is focused

on the money that is used to finance your business, such as loans. It also has to do with stock options and shareholders, and how that affects cash flow.

- Loans are added to your overall cash. However, your loan payments for the year are taken out of the overall cash.
- Dividends you pay out to shareholders obviously reduces your cash, while if you issue bonds or common stock, the issue is recorded as an influx of cash.

Lay out your statement of cash flows

Dividends	--	(16,000)
	59,724	(23,229)
CASH FLOWS FROM FINANCING ACTIVITIES		
Advances from (repayments to) shareholder	(180,200)	(150,000)
Acquisition of (repayment of) long-term debt	86,100	--
	(94,100)	(150,000)
NET INCREASE (DECREASE) IN CASH RESOURCES	81,026	(87,263)
CASH (DEFICIENCY) RESOURCES - Beginning of Year	(69,474)	17,789
CASH RESOURCES (DEFICIENCY) - End of Year	$ 11,552	$ (69,474)
Cash resources (deficiency) is comprised of:		
Cash	$ 11,552	$ --
Bank overdraft	--	(9,474)
Bank loan	--	(60,000)
	$ 11,552	$ (69,474)

accompanying summary of significant accounting policies and notes are an integral part of these financial statements.

6. Lay out your statement of cash flows. Start with the net income at the top, and move down through the three categories. It's best to keep the three categories separate, as then people reading the statement of cash flows can see where expenses are going in and out. Subtract and add cash as needed in each category, to reach your net increase or deficiency in cash for the year.

- Add in last year's cash. If you have any cash leftover from last year or you started out with a deficit, add that or subtract that to this year's cash.
- That will give you the total amount of cash you have on hand, also called your total cash resources.

How to Write a Balance Sheet

A balance sheet is a financial snapshot of an entity, either a business or an individual, at any given date. The "balance" comes from reporting assets and then balancing those assets with the liabilities and equity used to purchase them. Businesses must create balance sheets to analyze the financial health of the business, as well as to comply with their quarterly or annual accounting reports. While it may seem like another language to someone unfamiliar with accounting, a balance sheet is relatively easy to create. Use the following guide to create either a personal balance sheet for your household budget or a balance sheet for your business.

Method 1. Personal Balance Sheet

1. Choose a date for your balance sheet. Businesses are required to report their balance sheets on a certain date or dates each year. As an individual, however, you have much more freedom to choose your own date. Just be sure that the amounts that you gather for your debts and assets are all from the same date. List this date at the top of your balance sheet to remind you and also so that you can refer back to your balance sheet later.

- For regularity, you may choose to do a balance sheet at the end of the calendar year or twice per year at a set date. This will allow you to follow your net worth growth year-by-year.

2. Assemble your financial information. You will need records of your assets as well as your debt. Make sure you have your latest bank statements, the balance on any loans that you owe, and the current market value of your investments. You will also need to approximate the resale value of any valuable assets that you own, including your home, cars, and any valuable jewelry or household items.

- In general, list any valuable items that you own for which you could find a buyer and what that buyer might pay for the item. This can be determined by researching recent sales of similar items and noting the sale price. This is called the market value.
- In some cases, you may need to get a certified appraisal of larger, more valuable assets.

3. Set up your balance sheet. Unlike business balance sheets, which follow a preset formula, a personal balance sheet can follow any type of organization. In general though, it's a good idea to start by organizing your spreadsheet or paper into two rows or columns, one for assets and one for liabilities (debts). You can either do this by hand or use a spreadsheet program on the computer.

- There are also pre-made templates and editable online files that can be used to create a personal balance sheet. Try searching Google for "personal balance sheet template" and several options will show up.
- When judging the size of your balance sheet, know that your assets and liabilities will be listed by category and not by individual item. So if you have a large amount of valuable household items, know that these will be combined and listed as one line item on your balance sheet. Generally, a balance sheet should be no longer than one page.

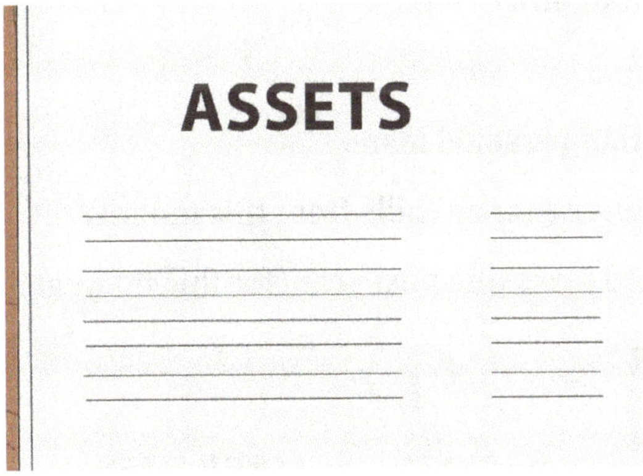

4. List your assets. In the first column or row, list your asset categories and their values. These include both financial assets as well as "hard" assets like cars and valuables. Listing these assets may require other tables in which you can sum the individual assets in each category. For example, if you have more than one car, you would combine the market value of your cars and list this on the balance sheet simply as "cars." The sum of these assets is your total assets. Include the following assets when making your balance sheet:

- Cash and account values in the bank (including checking, savings, money market, and certificate of deposit accounts)
- Investments (including stocks, real estate, mutual funds, college savings accounts)

- Any money owed to you (like a personal loan to a friend)
- Resale value of your home(s)
- Resale value of your vehicle(s)
- Resale value of personal property (such as jewelry and furniture)

5. List your liabilities. In the second column or row, list your liabilities as well as their value. These refer to any debts that you owe. Specifically, liabilities can include:

- Student loans
- Auto loans (what you currently owe)
- Credit card debt (this includes debt currently incurred even if you plan to pay it off at the end of your statement month)
- Mortgage balance
- The balance of any other personal loans
- Outstanding bill balances (unpaid bills from this month)
- Taxes due or estimated taxes due next year (for this tax year)

6. Total your assets and liabilities. To get an accurate picture of your net worth, start by totaling your columns or rows at the bottom of the balance sheet to get total assets and total liabilities. At this point, check to see that you haven't omitted anything from either category.

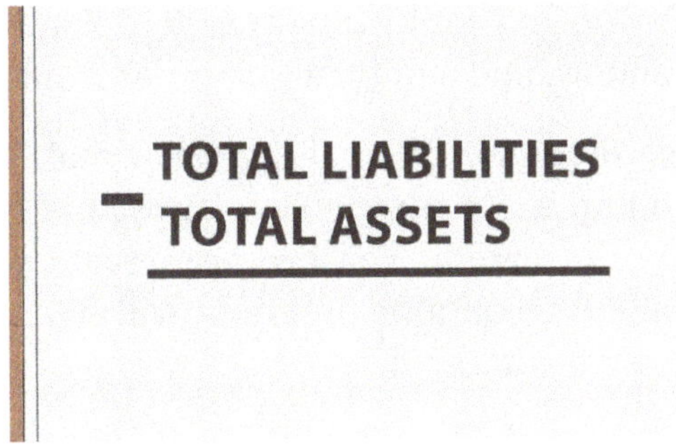

7. Subtract your total liabilities from your total assets. This will give you your net worth. This represents the total value of everything that you actually own. Your net worth will go up as your assets increase and your liabilities decrease. Use your balance sheet to budget your finances and achieve a higher net worth.

- Keep your balance sheet updated to track your progress towards your financial goals. Try to recalculate at least twice a year. This will help you see the big picture, so to speak.

Method 2. Business Balance Sheet

1. Understand the basics of the balance sheet. First, know that a balance sheet must always balance. That is, in the end, total assets must equal total liabilities plus owner's equity. Put another way, equity must equal the difference between total assets and total liabilities (Assets - Liabilities). Equity serves the same purpose at net worth does in the personal balance sheet.

- Businesses usually have to produce balance sheets as a part of annual reporting, but may also need one prepared to show potential lenders or investors.

2. Format your balance sheet. In the left column, you will be listing the assets. In the right column

you will list your liabilities at the top and equity underneath it. You can also list all the information in one column, with assets, liabilities, and equity in that order from top to bottom.

- Official business balance sheets all follow the same format. Try searching Google for "balance sheet template" to find a downloadable or printable balance sheet that you can fill out with your financial information. You can also create your own using a spreadsheet program. Additionally, some accounting programs will create balance sheets for your business, if you've chosen to invest in them.

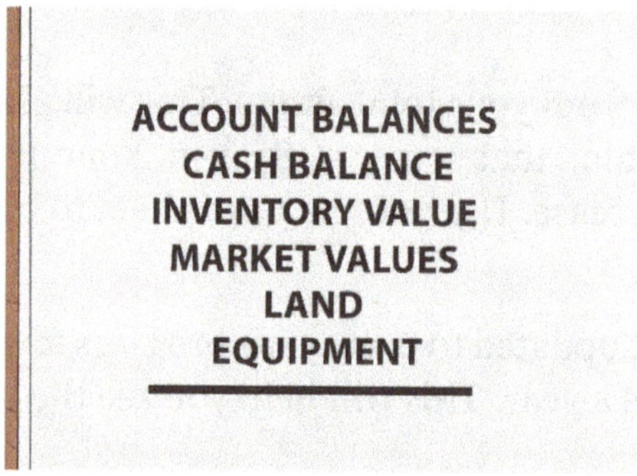

3. Gather your financial information. In order to create your balance sheet, you will need to have the current values of your assets, including account balances, cash balance, inventory value, and the market values of any investments, land, equipment, and other assets. You will also need to gather all of your liability balances, including any salaries owed, loan balances, and amounts owed to suppliers and utility companies. For equity, you will need to include any money contributed by the owners or investors in the company and a measure of retained earnings (profits reinvested in the company). Much of this information can be found in past financial statements and in the business general ledger.

- Keep in mind that this information will have to all be from the exact same date. For example a balance sheet for December 31st would total all balances through the end of business on that day.

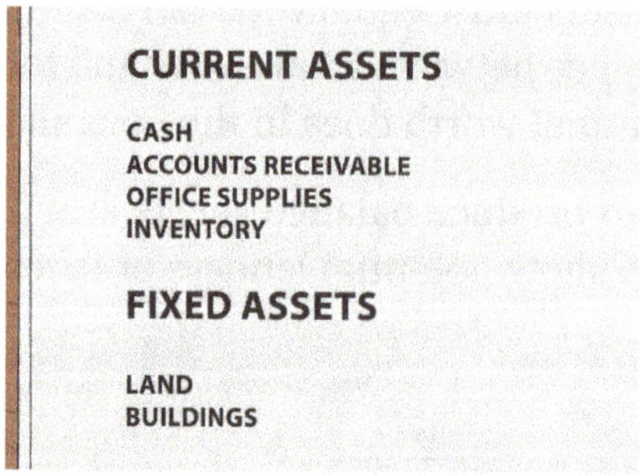

4. Record your assets. Assets are your company's resources. These include cash, accounts receivable, inventory, land, buildings, equipment, and more. These will be recorded at the top of your straight line balance sheet or on the left side of a columned one. A classified balance sheet breaks down assets into the following categories:

- Current assets. This includes cash (any money in bank accounts), accounts receivable (money owed to you), office supplies, inventory (even incomplete items), securities (stocks and bonds), prepaid expenses (like prepaid rent or utilities), and anything expected to be received or used up within a year.

- Fixed assets. These assets, also called long-term assets, are the revenue-producing items owned by the company, including land, buildings, machinery, vehicles, furniture, and any other objects that are expected to last longer than a year.
- You should subtract depreciation from these assets so you have an accurate picture of their worth. This reduces overvaluation of assets. For more information, see how to calculate depreciation on fixed assets.

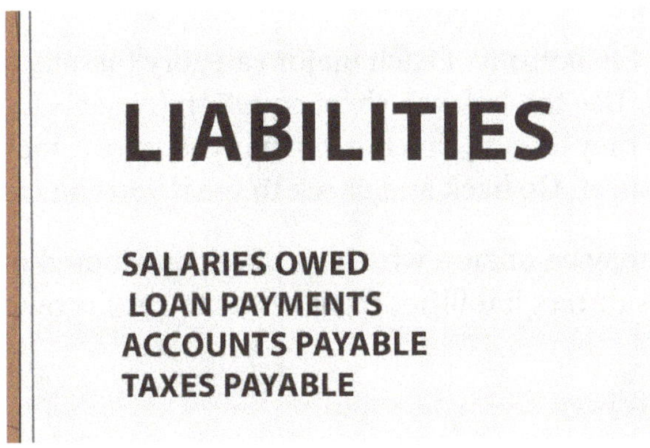

5. Record your liabilities. Liabilities are your company's debts. These include salaries owed, loan payments, and accounts payable. These will be recorded either under assets or on the right side of the balance sheet, depending on which balance sheet style you are using. They are split into two categories:

- Current liabilities. These are anything due within the next year, such as accounts payable (to suppliers or other companies), taxes, and payroll. It can also include the portion of long-term debt due within the next year.
- Long-term liabilities. This includes loans, mortgages, and leases that will be repaid more than one year from the date on the balance sheet.

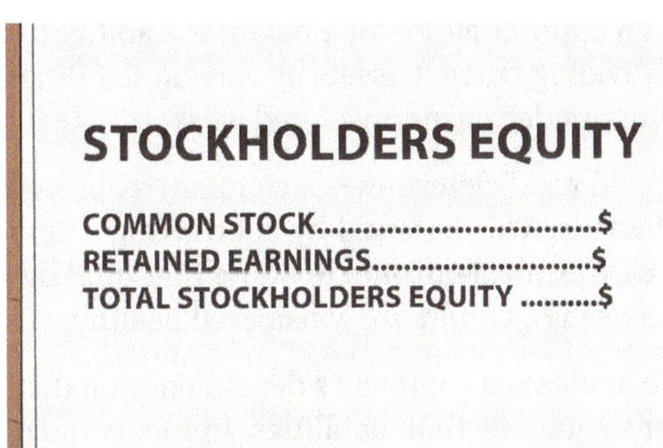

6. Record your equity. Owner's equity is how much the owners or stockholders have invested in the company. It also includes retained earnings, or net profits that are kept within the company. These will be recorded below liabilities, regardless of which balance sheet format you are using.

TOTAL ASSETS...$ TOTAL LIAB.& SE...$

7. Total your categories. At the bottom of each major category (assets, liabilities, and equity), sum each line item to get a total. Use the balance sheet equation (Assets=Liabilities + Equity) to check if your amounts balance. If they do not, this means that you've overlooked or incorrectly reported some part of your balance sheet. Go back and check to see if you can locate your mistake.

- In some cases, you may be unsure what you have contributed or retained to the company. In these cases, just subtract liabilities from assets to get the owner's equity.

$$\text{QUICK RATIO} = \frac{\text{CURRENT ASSETS-INVENTORY}}{\text{CURRENT LIABILITIES}}$$

8. Analyze your balance sheet. One you have a completed balance sheet, you can analyze it to determine certain important metrics that measure the financial health of your business. Specifically, there are four simple ratios that can be calculated from this information:

- The current ratio is an approximation of a business's ability to pay its current debts. Find the current ratio by dividing current assets by current liabilities. Values over 1 are considered stronger and those under 1 are considered weak.
- The quick ratio, or "acid test," determines a company's ability to pay its current liabilities with its most liquid assets. This is found by subtracting a company's inventory from the sum of its cash and cash equivalents and dividing that total by it's total current liabilities. Generally, results between 0.5 and 1 are considered healthy.
- The debt-worth ratio analyzes a company's dependency on debt. This measure is calculated by dividing owner's equity by total liabilities. In theory, no one result is better or worse here, but a business with a higher debt-worth ratio may be considered over-reliant on debt financing.
- The fixed-worth ratio determines how much the company has invested its own money in tangible assets. This is calculated by dividing total fixed assets by owner's equity. A low

ratio means a smaller investment in fixed assets and thus, less risk in case of business failure and liquidation.

Sample Balance Sheet

Year End <Date>

ASSETS		LIABILITIES	
Cash	$4,787.00	Mortgage balance	$38,000.00
Home, market value	$61,500.00	Bank Loan balance	$10,000.00
Apartment unit	$43,680.00	Auto Loan balance	$8,000.00
Car	$10,400.00	Credit Card, Visa	$13,688.90
Stocks	$9,000.00	Credit Card, Amex	$12,555.25
Government Bonds	$1,000.00	Total Liabilities	$82,244.15
Mutual Fund	$5,200.00		
Painting	$6,000.00		
Jewelry	$3,500.00		
Receivable	$650.00		
Total Assets	$145,717.00	Total Net Worth	$63,472.85

How to Make a Balance Sheet for Accounting

Part 1. Setting Up Your Balance Sheet

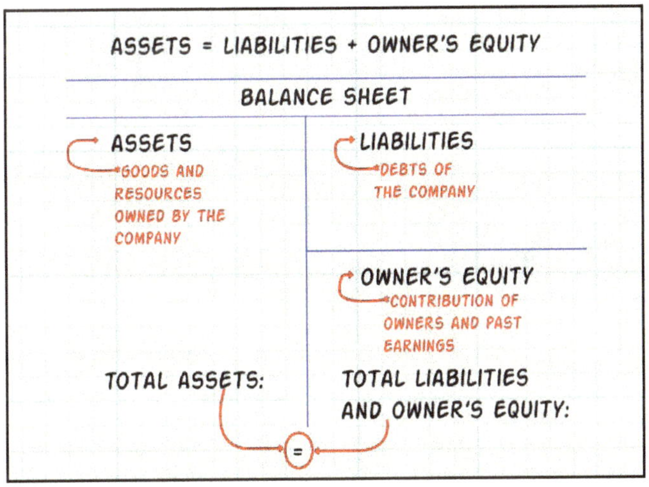

1. Use the basic accounting equation to make a balance sheets. This is Assets = Liabilities + Owner's Equity. Thus, a balance sheet has three sections: Assets, which are the resources owned; Liabilities, which are the company's debts; and Owner's Equity, which is contributions by shareholders and the company's earnings. The information needed to complete a balance sheet can be found on the company's general ledger where all financial transactions for a particular period will have been recorded.

- In a balance sheet, the total sum of assets must equal the sum of liabilities and owner's equity.
- The asset accounts represent all the goods and resources that a company owns. The liability portion represents all of its debts. The equity portion represents contributions by owners (shareholders) and past earnings. Theoretically, all the assets of the company are either financed by borrowing, which is associated with the liability accounts, or are financed by past earnings and contributions from owners, which are associated with equity.

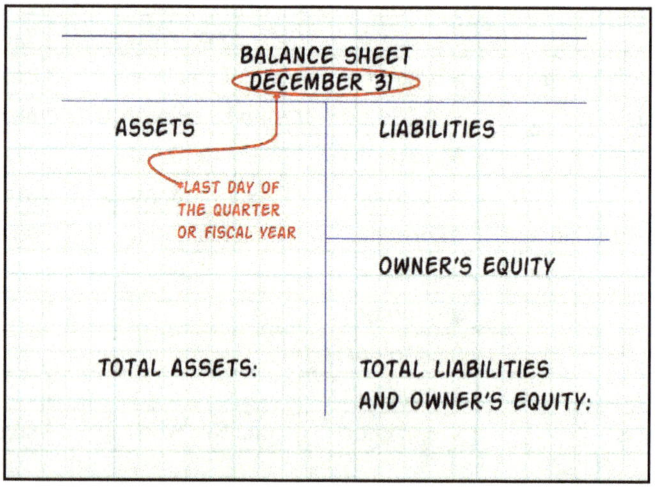

2. Choose the date for the balance sheet. The balance sheet is created to show the assets, liabilities, and equity of a company on a specific day of the year. Usually companies prepare an official balance sheet quarterly (the last day of March, June, September and December, for example) and at the end of their fiscal year (such as December 31) but it can be done at any time.

- You might not finish putting together the balance sheet until several weeks after the end of the fiscal year (Dec. 31 for example), but your data collection end date and balance sheet date would still be December 31.

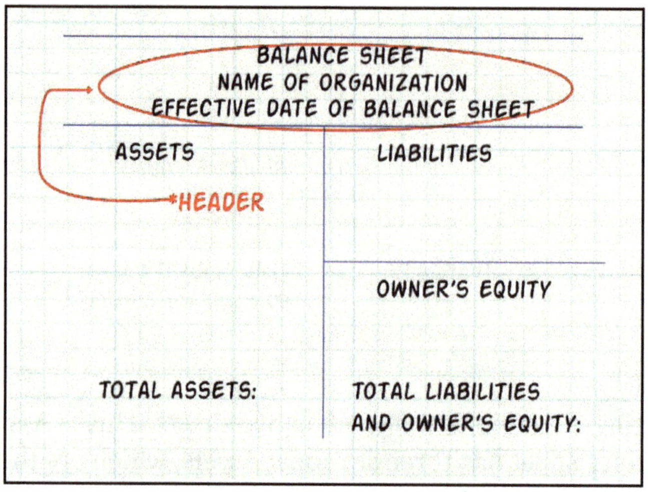

3. Prepare the header of the balance sheet. Use the title "Balance Sheet," at the top of the page. Beneath it, list the name of the organization, and the effective date of the balance sheet (the last day of the quarter or fiscal year).

Part 2. Preparing the Assets Section

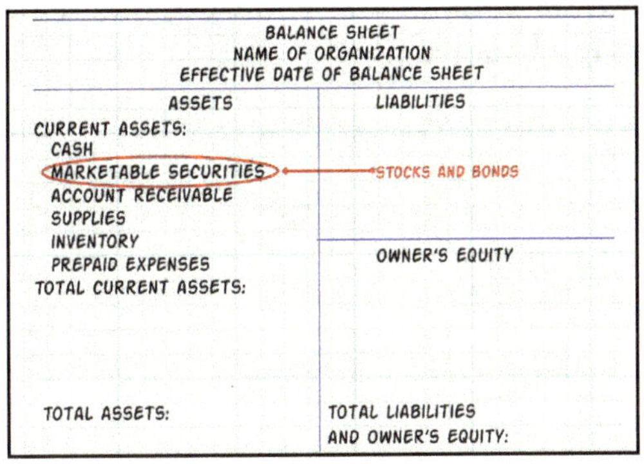

1. List all current assets. Current assets are assets that can turn into cash within one year of the balance sheet date. They are listed in order of relative liquidity, in other words how easily they could be converted into cash. Common current asset accounts include cash, marketable securities (such as stocks, bonds, etc.), accounts receivable, supplies, inventory, and prepaid expenses (such as prepaid insurance, prepaid rent, etc.).

- Include a subtotal of the current assets accounts and call it "Total Current Assets."

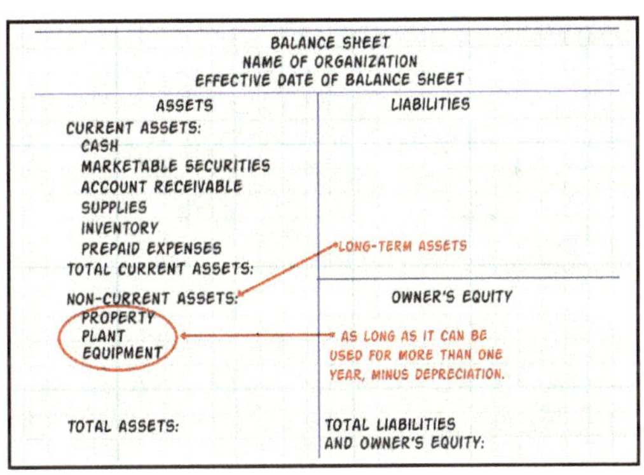

2. List all non-current assets, also known as long-term assets. Non-current assets are defined as a company's value of property, plant, and equipment that can be used for more than 1 year, minus depreciation. The general ledge will indicate the current value of long-term assets.

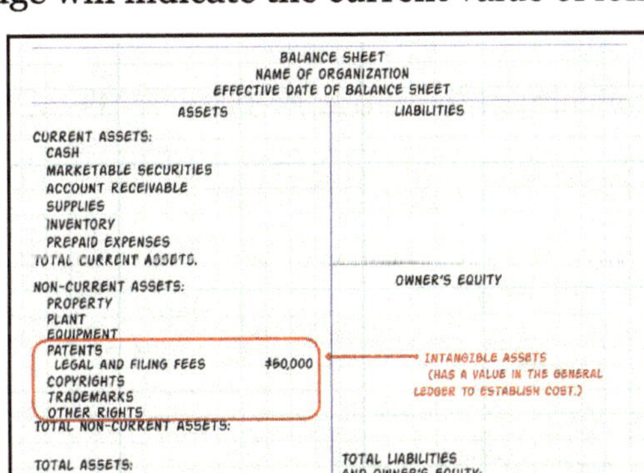

3. Include any intangible assets. These are also considered non-current. Intangible assets refer to non-monetary assets that have no physical substance and will last more than 1 year. These include patents, copyrights, trademarks, and other rights.

- Non-tangible assets will have a value in the general ledger to establish cost. For example, if legal and filing fees for patents totaled $50,000, that is the cost that will appear on the company ledger and on the balance sheet.
- Include a subtotal of the non-current assets and call it "Total Non-Current Assets."

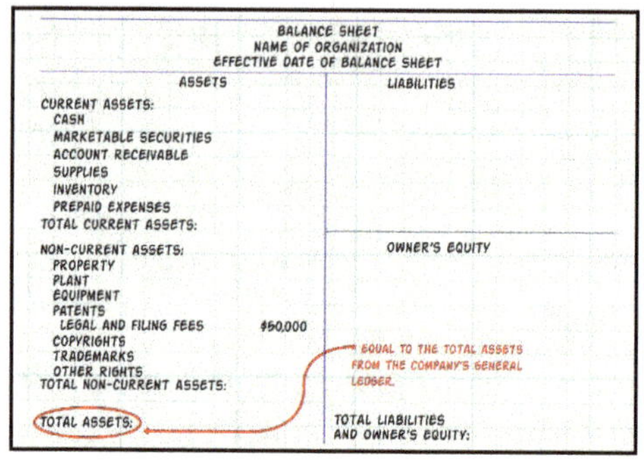

4. Add up the current and non-current assets totals and label this amount "Total Assets." Here, check that the total assets per your balance sheet are equal to the total assets from the company's general ledger. Investigate and resolve any differences you find.

Part 3. Preparing the Liabilities Section

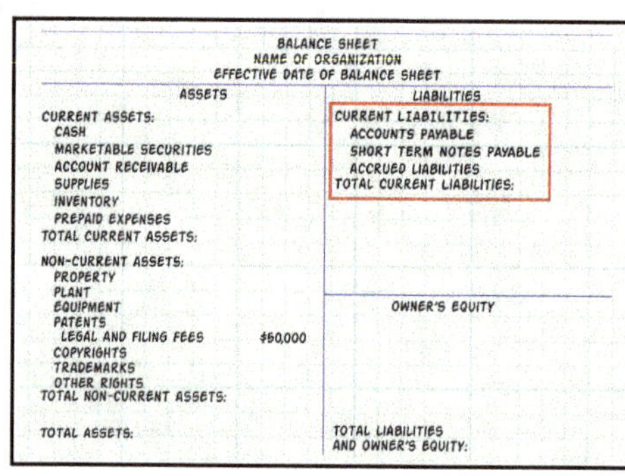

1. Determine current liabilities. Current liabilities are liabilities that are due within one year of the balance sheet date. Common current liabilities accounts include: accounts payable, short-term notes payable, and accrued liabilities.

- Include a subtotal of the current liabilities and title it "Total Current Liabilities."

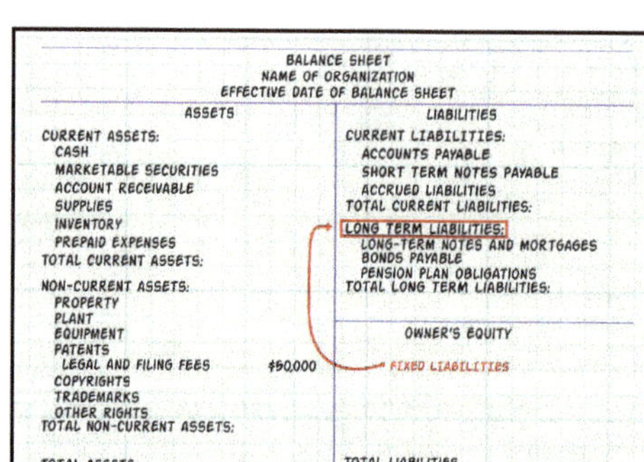

2. Calculate all long-term liabilities, also known as fixed liabilities. These are any liabilities that

will not be settled within one year. Long-term liabilities include: long-term notes and mortgages, bonds payable, and pension plan obligations.

- Include a subtotal of long-term liabilities and label this line "Total Long-term Liabilities."

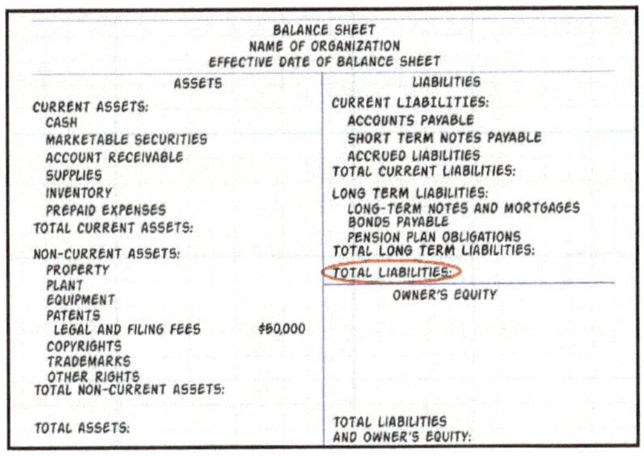

3. Add the current liabilities subtotal to the long-term liabilities subtotal. Label this line "Total Liabilities." The balance for total liabilities will be shown on the second part of your balance sheet and will be added to the owner's equity.

Part 4. Calculating Owner's Equity and Totals

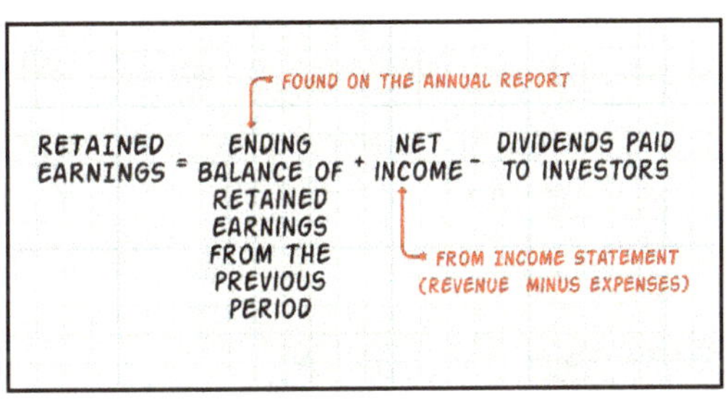

1. Calculate Retained Earnings. Retained earnings are the amount of profit a company has earned for a particular time period. First find the ending balance of retained earnings from the previous period (found on the annual report), add the net income (revenue minus expenses) from your Income Statement, deduct dividends paid to investors, and get the final total for current retained earnings.

- The Statement of Retained Earnings will not be listed on your balance sheet but will help you calculate owner's equity.

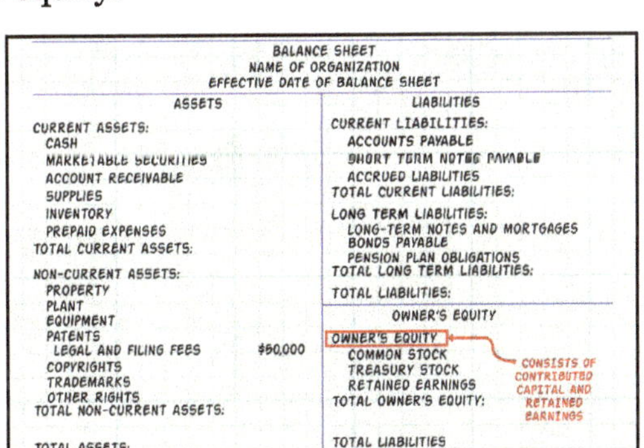

2. Calculate the owner's equity. Equity consists of contributed capital (money invested) and

retained earnings (historical sum of profits and losses). Here, make a list of all the equity accounts like common stock, treasury stock, and the retained earnings number from Step 1.

- Once all the equity accounts are listed, sum them and add the caption "Total Owner's Equity."

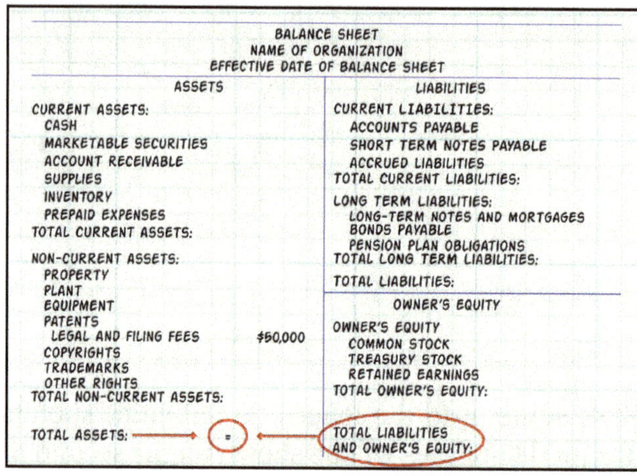

BALANCE SHEET
NAME OF ORGANIZATION
EFFECTIVE DATE OF BALANCE SHEET

ASSETS		LIABILITIES
CURRENT ASSETS:		CURRENT LIABILITIES:
CASH		ACCOUNTS PAYABLE
MARKETABLE SECURITIES		SHORT TERM NOTES PAYABLE
ACCOUNT RECEIVABLE		ACCRUED LIABILITIES
SUPPLIES		TOTAL CURRENT LIABILITIES:
INVENTORY		LONG TERM LIABILITIES:
PREPAID EXPENSES		LONG-TERM NOTES AND MORTGAGES
TOTAL CURRENT ASSETS:		BONDS PAYABLE
NON-CURRENT ASSETS:		PENSION PLAN OBLIGATIONS
PROPERTY		TOTAL LONG TERM LIABILITIES:
PLANT		TOTAL LIABILITIES:
EQUIPMENT		OWNER'S EQUITY
PATENTS		OWNER'S EQUITY
LEGAL AND FILING FEES	$50,000	COMMON STOCK
COPYRIGHTS		TREASURY STOCK
TRADEMARKS		RETAINED EARNINGS
OTHER RIGHTS		TOTAL OWNER'S EQUITY:
TOTAL NON-CURRENT ASSETS:		
TOTAL ASSETS:	=	TOTAL LIABILITIES AND OWNER'S EQUITY:

3. Add the "Total Liabilities" and "Total Owner's Equity" figures. Title the sum "Total Liabilities and Owner's Equity." The balance sheet has been correctly prepared if "Total Assets" and "Total Liabilities and Owner's Equity" are equal. If this is the case, then your balance sheet is now complete.

- If balance sheet does not balance, double check your work. You may have omitted, duplicated, or miscategorized one of your accounts. Also double check your retained earnings balance, as this is a common problem area.

How to Read a Balance Sheet

Part 1. Calculating your Assets

1. Know that assets are anything of value owned by the company. Assets are valuable resources that you own or control, from cash and manufacturing equipment to the company car. They are sometimes called "debits." In a column labeled "Assets," list each asset and its worth.

- The easiest asset to calculate is cash. How much money could your business spend at any moment without a loan or credit card? Write this down as "Cash."

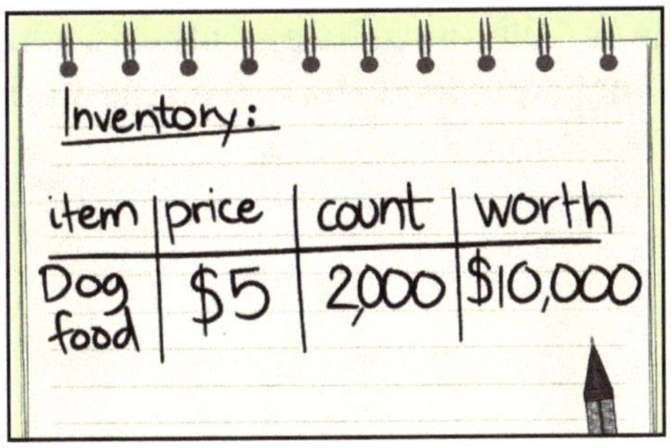

2. Calculate how much money your inventory is worth. Inventory is the total supply of your product. If I sell dog food, for instance, my inventory would be every bag of food in my stores. Calculate how much money you would make if you sold every single bag at normal price.

- For example, if I sell each bag for $5, and I have 2,000 bags in my warehouse, my inventory is worth $10,000.

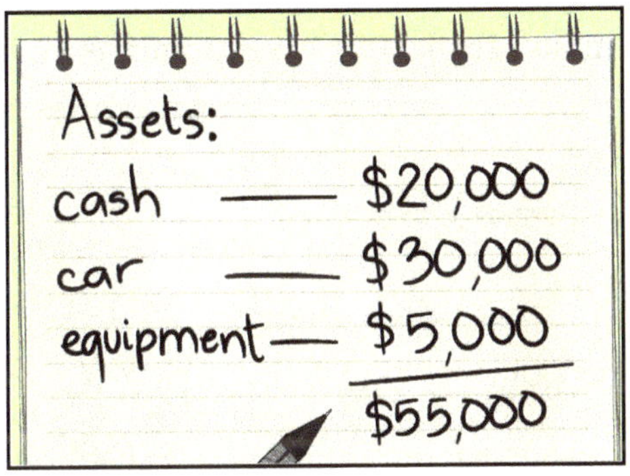

3. Calculate the worth of your equipment. Your business's property, manufacturing plant and equipment are all essential to your business, but could be sold. If you are still paying the mortgage on a $200,000 property, for example, you would still list a $200,000 property under assets.

- If the market value for my high-end food processor, oven, and refrigerator is $5,000, I would note $5,000 under "equipment."
- If you rent your equipment or space, and could not sell, then it is not an asset.

4. Include any money you are owed as "Account Receivable." When someone owes you money you

can claim it as an asset, even if you do not know when you will be paid back. This is "accounts receivable," or "A/R," because you can count on receiving the money.

- Many businesses include an "allowance" in parenthesis, admitting that some debts may not be paid back. If I know that a pet food store owed me $1,000 and went out of business, I might note this next to "Accounts Receivable."

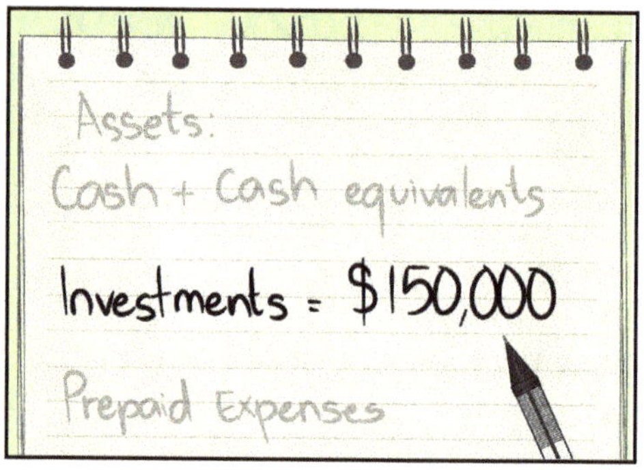

5. Note the amount of money in investments. Though this is not accessed as readily as cash, any investments a business makes are expected return a profit are and are thus assets. Write down the amount you expect to yield (or make) from your investment as an asset.

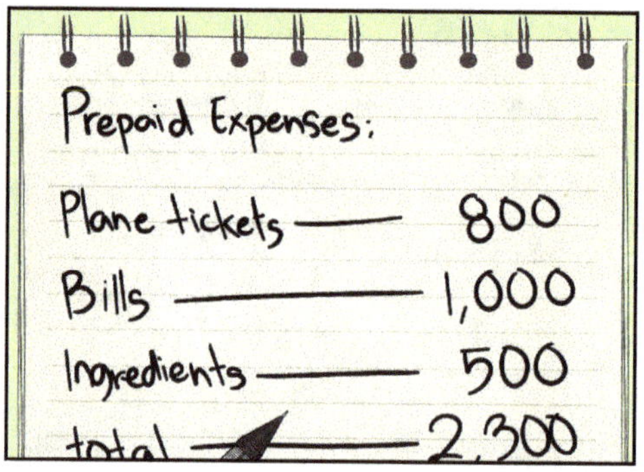

6. Consider pre-paid expenses as assets. If you've paid your bills in advance, whether buying your ingredients for 6 months in bulk or purchasing plane tickets for next year's trade conference, you can list these as assets under "pre-paid expenses." While you usually can't sell them, they represent money you will not have to spend again, meaning you can save more of your profits later on.

7. Intangibles that cannot be easily sold, like brands, trademarks, and patents, are not assets. These cannot be readily valued and thus are arbitrary figures. Intangibles may be worth a great amount

of money, but they are not added to a balance sheet. Their value lies in their ability to generate a profit and are listed in an income statement.

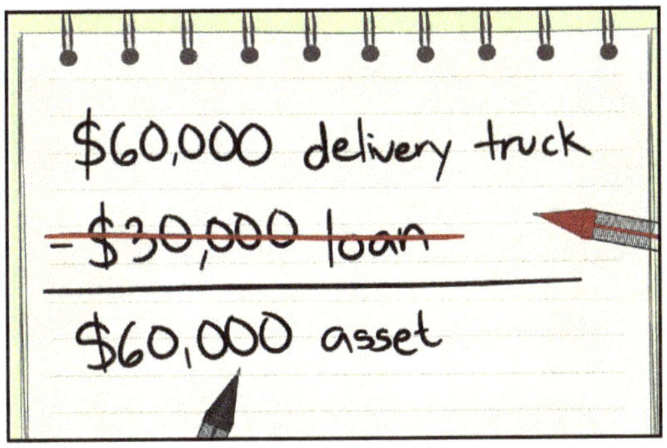

8. Know that even partial ownership of something makes it an asset. You must list the full worth of assets you don't fully own. For example, -- if you buy a delivery truck worth $60,000, but took out a loan for $30,000 to pay for it, you must still list the truck as an asset worth $60,000.

- This is true for mortgages too -- no matter how much money I still owe on a $500,000 factory, that factory is still a $500,000 asset for my business.

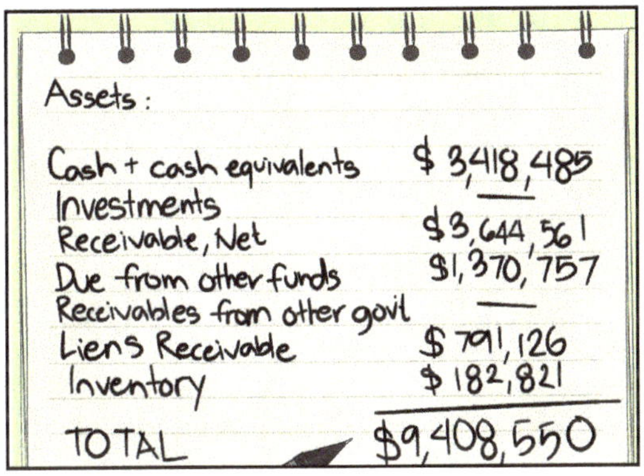

8. List all your assets on one side of a balance sheet and add them together. This number represents your business's total assets, or everything of value in your company.

Part 2. Calculating Total Liability

1. Understand that liability represents your company's debts. Liabilities are obligations of the business to pay something or someone in the future. It includes credit card debt, mortgage payments, business expenses, loans, and bills.

- Liability is the money that you turn into assets -- for example, you need to take out a loan build a factory. The loan is the liability, the factory is the asset.

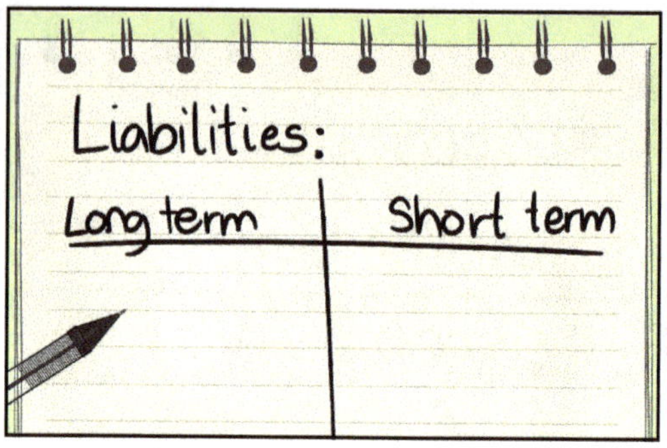

2. Make columns on your balance sheet for short-term and long-term liability. Separating debts that need to be paid soon from those that can wait helps show the stability of your company. If you owe a lot of credit-card debt, for example, you need to find a way to pay it off before a 30-year mortgage.

- If you need to pay the debt within one year it is short-term, or "current," liability. Anything else is long-term.

3. Calculate your 'accounts payable," or the debts you owe to other businesses. An example would be buying ingredients from a company regularly, but paying them back after you've sold your product. These are usually due within one year and are thus "short-term liabilities."

4. Calculate any loans or mortgages, and interest due. Generally, a loan is a long-term liability, but regular interest payments are short-term.

- You do not mark the full loan as liability, only the amount you still owe.

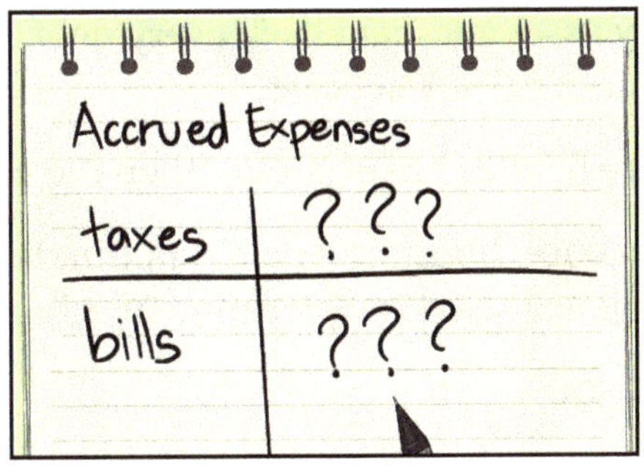

5. Note any "accrued expenses," like taxes or bills. These are usually the expenses that you know you have to pay but haven't been charged yet. Often this is extrapolated from past years' expenses. If, for example, you know that your equipment needs maintenance and repair every year, you can mark it on your balance sheet now to plan for the future.

- Bills, insurance, and income tax are all possible accrued expenses.

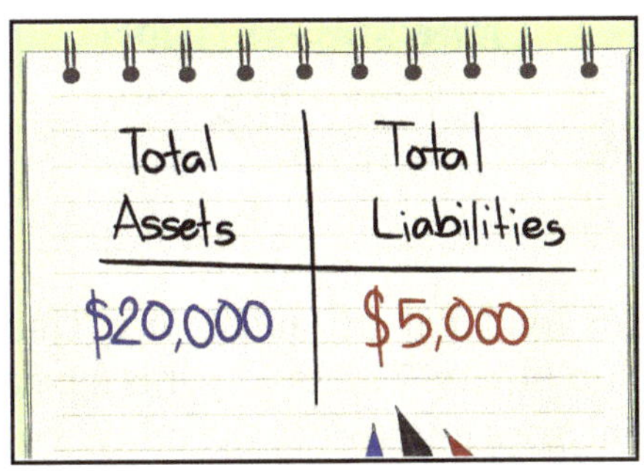

6. List all your liability next to your assets. Once you have noted every debt, expense, and liability, list it on your balance sheet. Many business put it next to the assets so they can easily compare the two numbers. #Add up your current, long-term, and total liability. This is your total liability, or every debt your business owes.

- Be thorough when listing liability -- suddenly realizing you missed a large payment or debt can derail your company if you are not careful.

Part 3. Making Sense of Your Balance Sheet

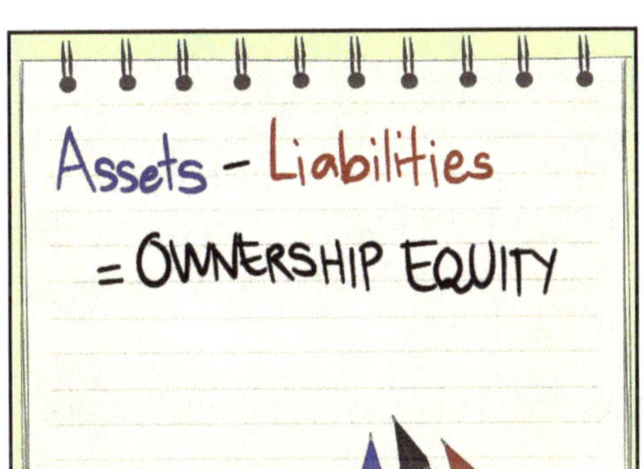

1. Subtract your liability from your assets to find "ownership equity." Equity is the amount of money the owners (you, shareholders, etc.) have invested in the business. It represents how much the

company is worth if it sold every asset and paid back every debt. Equity is how much money you would make if you sold the business at its exact cost.

- If equity is negative (more liability than assets), then the company is in debt.
- *Example:* I bought a $200,000 house and paid $25,000 for it up front. I take out a loan for $175,000. I could us a balance sheet to determine my Home Equity:
    - Assets: House, $200,000
    - Liability: Mortgage, $175,000.
    - Home Equity: Assets - Liability = $25,000.

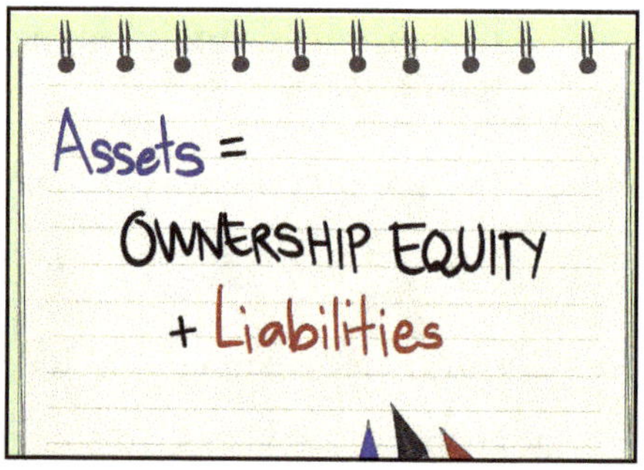

2. Remember that assets ALWAYS equal liability and equity. This is an iron-clad rule of accounting: Assets = Liability + Ownership Equity. This is why it is a balance sheet -- because both sides are always balanced. So, if one side goes up, so does the other. For example, if my company gets a tax return of $2,500, and I don't owe any more money because of it, than my equity just went up $2,500. This way the sheet stays "balanced."

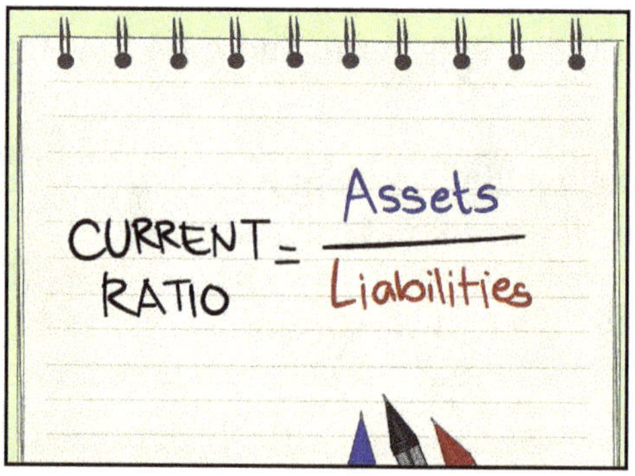

3. Calculate the "current ratio" to determine how much money a company can spare for growth. To do so, divide the assets by the current liability. This will return a number, usually between .5 and 2, that tells you how many spare assets the company has to grow or pay back debt. Generally, a current ratio above above 1.5 is a good goal.

- If this ratio is below 1 then the company is spending more money on short-term debt than it has saved in assets.
- If my dog food company has $20,000 in assets and owes $10,000 in liability, my current ratio would be 2. This means that I have twice as much money I could spend as I owe. Remember, however, that not all assets are easily converted into cash.

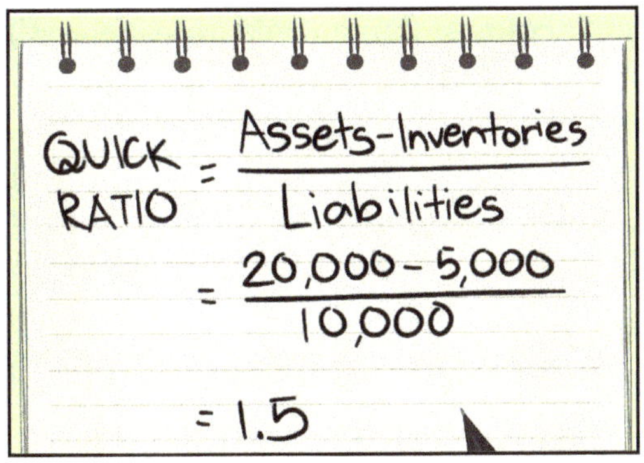

4. Calculate the "quick ratio" to determine a company's finances if it stopped making sales. Because inventory is often sold for a different price than it is worth (during a 50% off sale, for example) it can inflate your assets and make the company look stronger than it is. The quick rate subtracts inventory from assets, then divides that number by the current liability.

- The quick ratio is helpful for determining the health of a company that may fluctuate sales numbers depending on current trends, like fashion or music sellers.
- Healthy businesses will have a quick ratio greater than one.
- If my dog food company has $20,000 in assets, but $5,000 of those assets are the projected sales of kibble, then I would assume I have only $15,000 in assets. I could then divide by my total liability to find the quick ratio.

5. Update you balance sheet 1-4 times a year. The balance sheet provides a snapshot of your companies health, and while it may help prepare for the future, it does not predict it. You need to have accurate balance sheets often to help you manage debt, convert assets into growth, and see detect financial problems before they become too large to manage.

- Commonly, businesses will prepare quarterly balance sheets-- or one every 3 months.

How to Write an Income Statement

An income statement is a key financial document in business. It shows the profitability of a company over a specific period of time. The following guide shows you how to prepare a simple multi-step income statement. A multi-step income statement separates operating income and expenses from non-operating items.

Part 1. Setting Up Your Income Statement

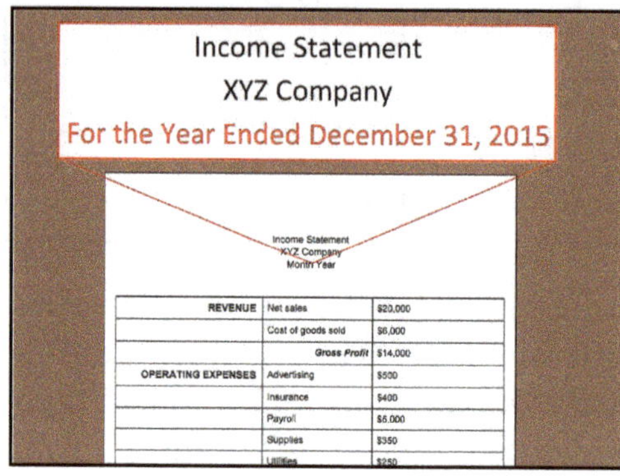

1. Choose a time period for your income statement. Income statements measure revenues and expenses during a certain period of time and are typically generated on a monthly, quarterly, or annual basis.

- Businesses that are publicly traded must generate income statements on quarterly and annual basis to file with the Securities and Exchange Commission.
- Businesses also generate income statements on a periodic basis to identify business trends and evaluate financial results.

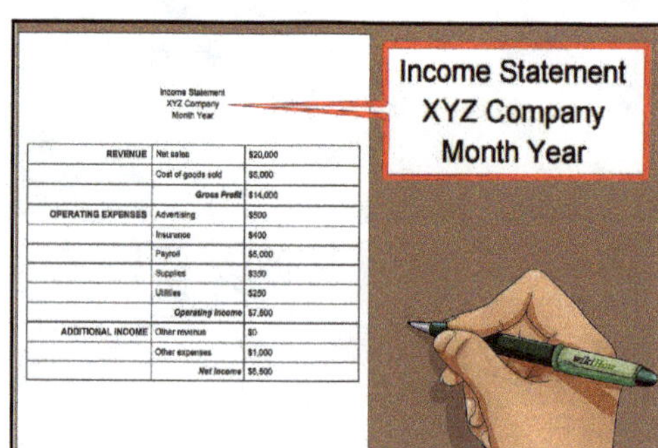

2. Format the income statement header. At the top of the document, write the name of the company. On the line directly beneath the company name, write "Income Statement." On the next line, write the period of time that the income statement covers.

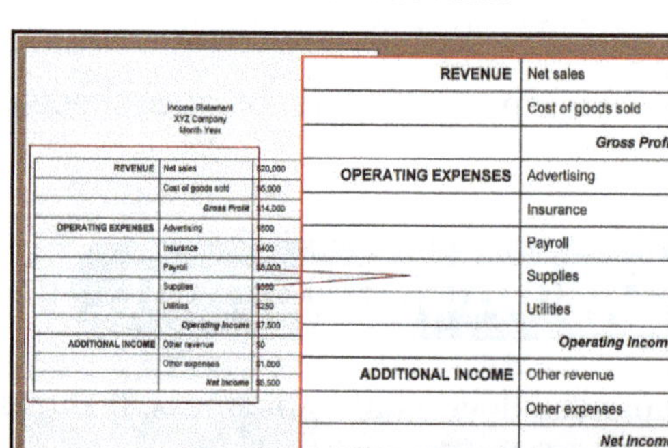

3. Format the body of the income statement. Income statements have four distinct sections.
   - The first section of the income statement calculates gross profit from sales revenue and cost of goods sold.
   - The second section calculates operating income from gross profit and operating expenses.
   - The third section calculates non-operating income based on non-operating revenues and expenses.
   - The fourth section calculates net income using all revenue and expense information.

Part 2. Preparing the Gross Profit Section

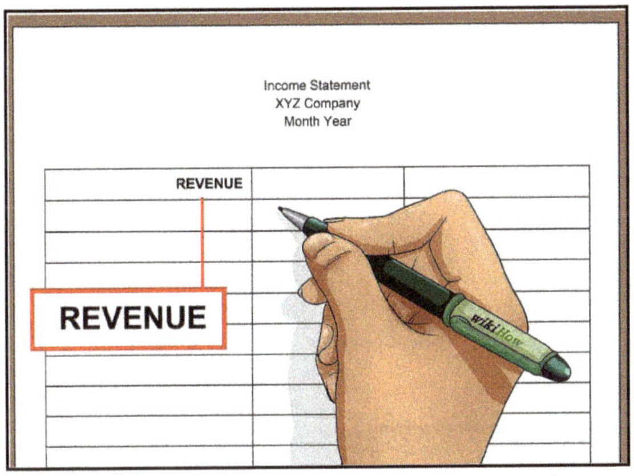

1. Write "Sales revenue" below the income statement header. List sales revenue for the period.
   - Sales revenue includes all revenue earned from the sale of goods and services, regardless of whether or not the cash has been collected.
   - For example, say that you sold 10,000 units of inventory for $5 a piece. You would record sales revenue of $50,000, even if your customers haven't all paid you yet.

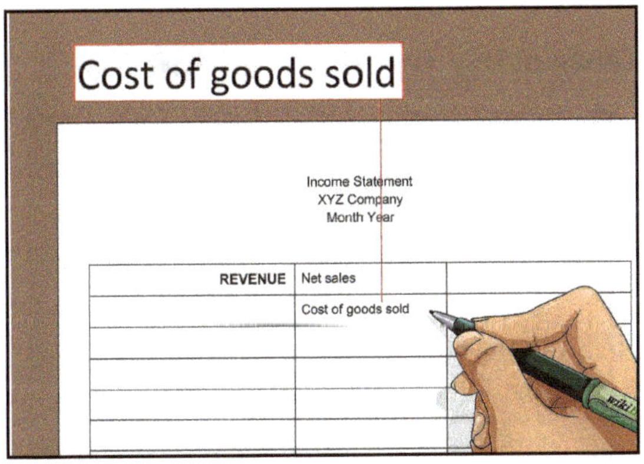

2. Write "Cost of goods sold" below "Sales revenue." List cost of goods sold for the period.
   - Cost of goods sold is comprised of the direct labor, direct materials, and manufacturing overhead expense you incurred to create the inventory that you sold. If you're a reseller, cost of goods sold is typically the price that you paid to purchase the inventory.

- For example, if you sold 10,000 units of inventory during the period and paid an average of $2 for each unit, you would record $20,000 of cost of goods sold.

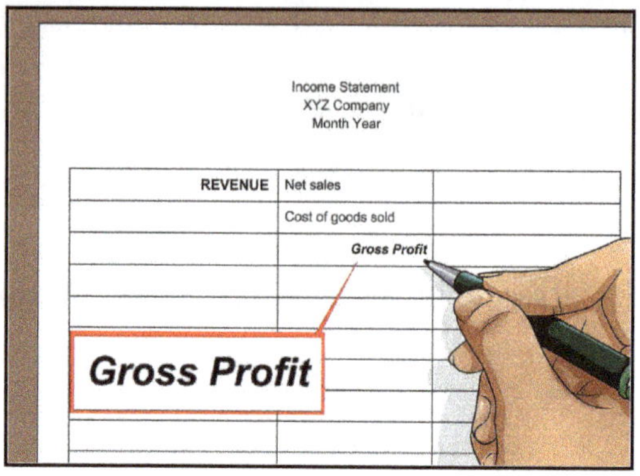

3. Label the next line "Gross profit." Gross profit represents how much profit a company earns from selling products before they pay for selling, general, and administrative expenses.

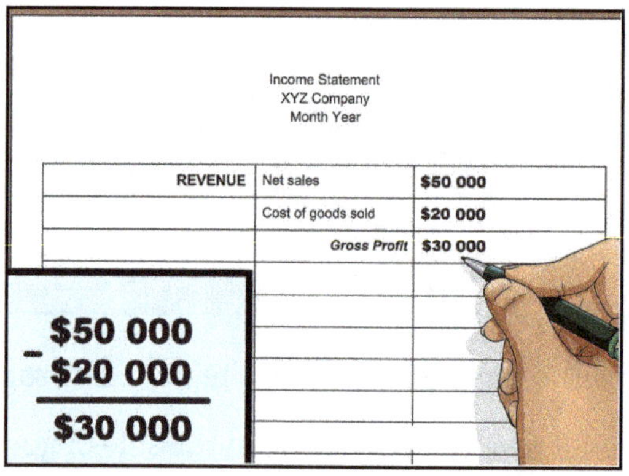

4. Subtract cost of goods sold from sales revenue. The resulting value is gross profit for the period. For example, if sales revenue is $50,000 and cost of goods sold is $20,000, you would record gross profit of $30,000 on the income statement.

Part 3. Preparing the Operating Income Section

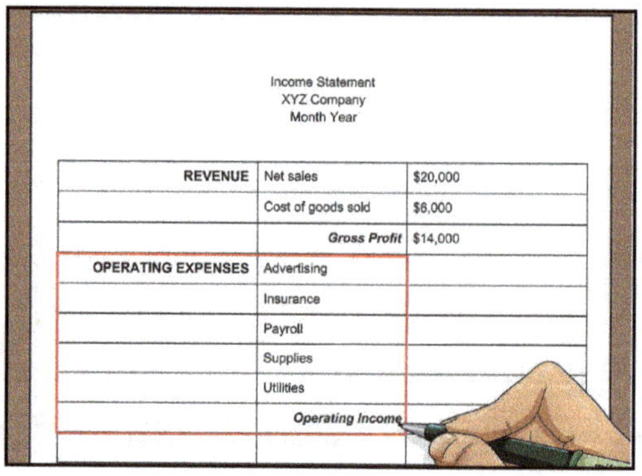

1. Write all the types of operating expenses the business has. Operating expenses are expenses that directly relate to business administration. Next to each line item, list the amount of expense incurred during the period.

- Common operating expenses include salary and wages for those employees not directly involved in the product of goods, rent, insurance, office supplies, professional fees, utilities, transportation expense, marketing, depreciation, and property taxes. Direct labor has already been deducted from the Cost of Goods.
- Non-cash expenses such as depreciation and amortization should also be included. Depreciation and amortization are both methods that reduce the recorded cost of assets. Depreciation is most commonly calculated using a straight line method, which is gradually reducing the cost of a tangible asset over its useful life. Amortization is used for intangible assets and is calculated similarly to depreciation.
- If the business has a large variety of expenses, you can group similar line items into one category to save space. For example, you can create an "Employee compensation" line item that includes salaries, health insurance premiums, retirement benefits, payroll taxes, worker's compensation, and payroll processing fees.

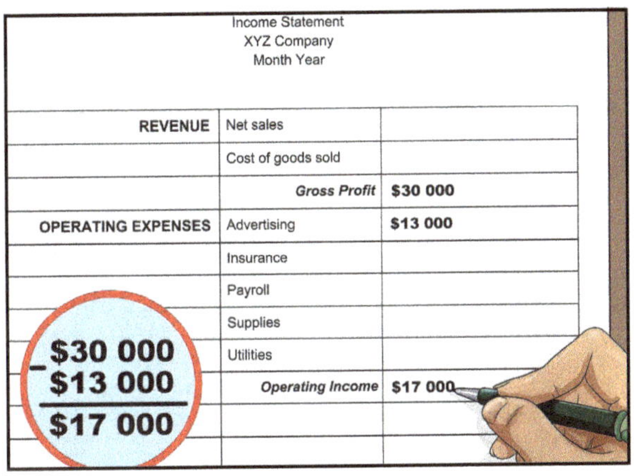

2. Sum each operating expense line item to determine total operating expenses. Subtract total operating expenses from gross profit. The resulting value is operating income for the period. For example, if total operating expenses are $13,000 and gross profit is $30,000, operating income is $17,000.

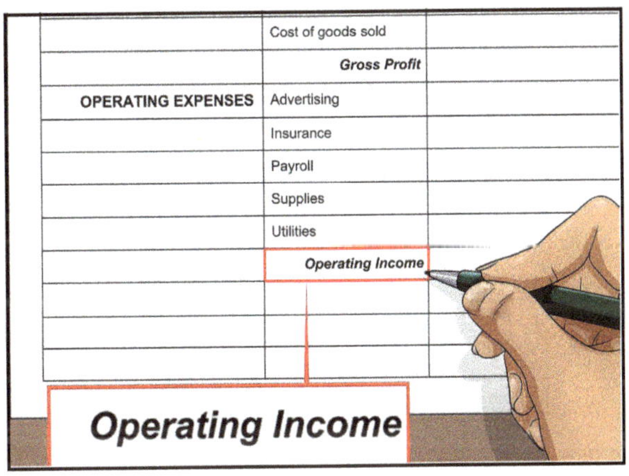

3. Label the next line "Operating income." Operating income represents the income that a business earned from its normal, core business functions.

Part 4. Preparing the Non-operating Income Section

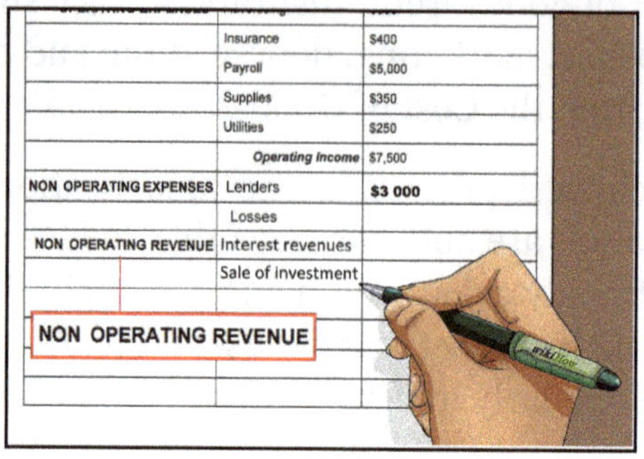

1. Write all the types of non-operating revenues the business has. Non-operating revenues are revenues that don't directly relate to business operations, sales, and production. These revenues are from activities that are different or peripheral to normal operations. Next to each line item, list the amount of revenue incurred during the period.

   - Common non-operating revenues include interest revenues and gains from the sale of investments and securities. These items add to the income of the enterprise while expenses reduce income.

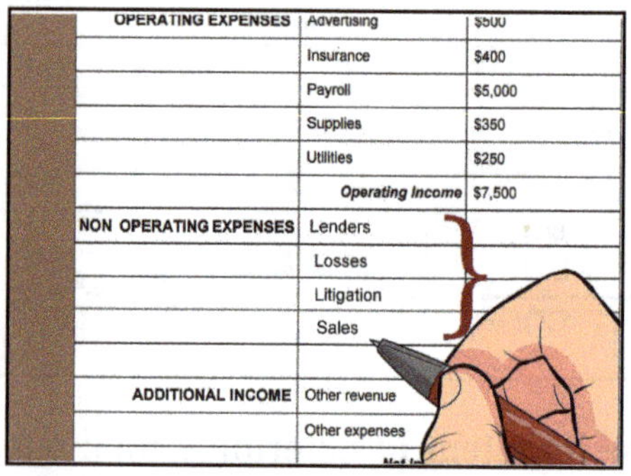

2. Write all the types of non-operating expenses the business has. Non-operating expenses also don't directly relate to business operation or sales. Next to each line item, list the amount of expense incurred during the period.

   - Common non-operating expenses include interest expense paid to lenders, losses from the sale of investments, and losses from litigation.

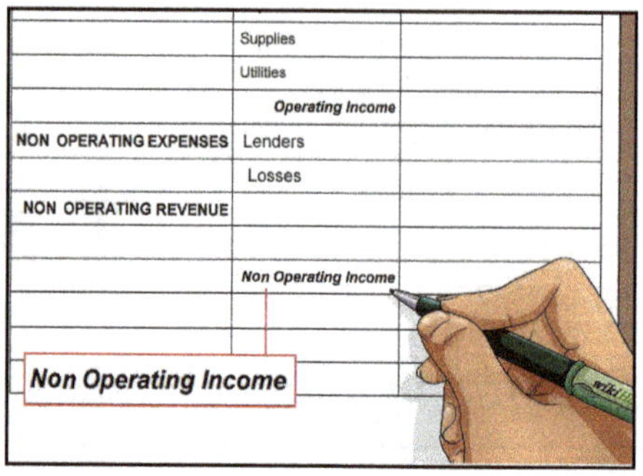

3. Label the next line "Non-operating income." Non-operating income represents income that didn't come from core operations.

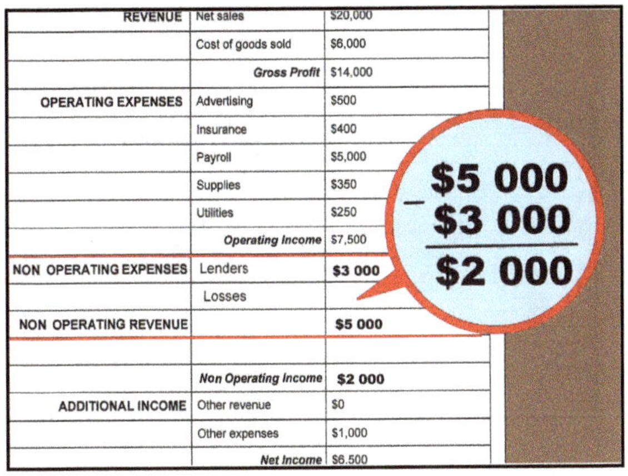

4. Subtract non-operating expenses from non-operating revenues. The resulting figure is non-operating income for the period. For example, if non-operating revenue is $5,000 and non-operating expenses are $3,000, non-operating income is $2,000.

Part 5. Preparing the Net Income Section

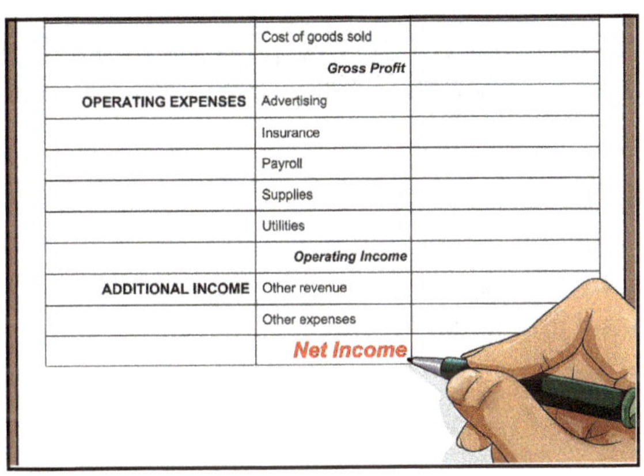

1. Label the next line "Net income." Net income represents how much income is left over from revenue after accounting for all expense

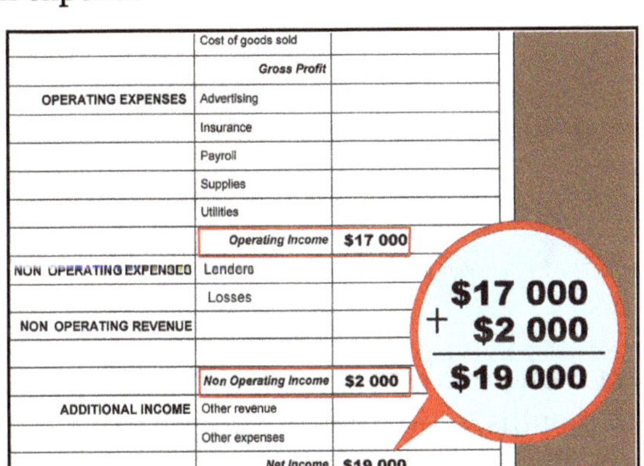

2. Add non-operating income to operating income. The resulting value is net income for the period. In this example, net income would be $17,000 of operating income and $2,000 of non-operating income for a total of $19,000.

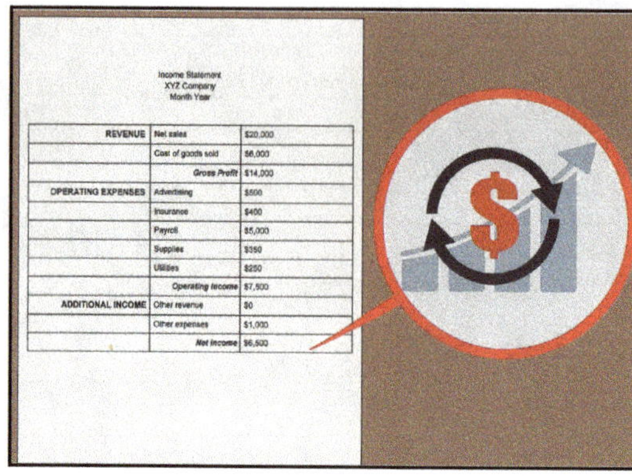

3. Transfer the balance of net income to retained earnings. This resets the balance of net income for the next accounting period.

- Retained earnings can be used to pay dividends to owners or be reinvested in business activities.

How to Prepare a Profit and Loss Statement

A profit and loss statement provides information about your business's past activities, and is an essential document that must be created as part of your financial reporting. You may need to create one if, for example, you're applying for a small business loan. While you can find templates to use to prepare a profit and loss statement, it's also a fairly simple document that you can create yourself using your business's basic financial records.

Part 1. Calculating Revenue

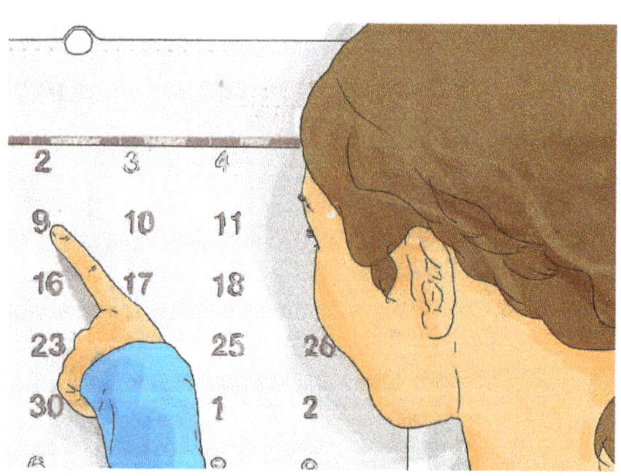

1. Choose the time period you want your report to cover. You may want to create a profit and loss statement to cover only a few months, or to cover an entire year of operations. If you're preparing the statement for a third party, they may dictate the period of time the statement should cover.

- A profit and loss statement typically should cover at least one quarter to convey any significant degree of helpful information.

- At the same time, a profit and loss statement that covers more than a 12-month period typically will have too much data to be particularly useful.

2. Adjust your data accordingly. A profit and loss statement that covers only a brief period of time, such as three months or one quarter, can have a lot more detail than one that covers an entire year of operations.

- The longer the period of time you cover, the less detailed your profit and loss statement should be. For example, if you're preparing a profit and loss statement covering the last six months, you may want to include income and expense totals for each month.

However, if your profit and loss statement covers an entire year, it may be more helpful to break that year down into quarters, rather than individual months.

3. Gather documentation of sales figures and other revenue. To prepare your profit and loss statement, you'll need raw figures for all income your business has earned during the period the statement will cover, including any gains from assets.

- If you don't have a bookkeeper or use accounting software, gathering these documents may present a challenge.
- However, keep in mind that if you haven't recorded income, you'll not only have trouble creating this statement, you'll also have problems when you're preparing your taxes.
- Divide your income into general categories so you can determine how much money your business is bringing in for each avenue of your operations.

- You also want to keep non-operating income, such as capital gains, separate from your operating income.
- Financial records are important, so if you run across any gaps in your record-keeping while you're gathering income information to complete your statement, make a note to fix the problem as soon as possible.

4. Total your income over the chosen period. Typically you'll want to include totals for smaller periods of time, such as months or quarters, in addition to the ultimate total income for the entirety of the period covered by the statement.

- You'll want totals in each category as well as the total of all income over the given period and each division of that period.
- For example, if you have income in three categories and your profit and loss statement is covering three months, you'll want a total for income in each category in each month, as well as totals for each category of income over the entire quarter.
- Then, you'll want to total income in each category for the entire quarter, along with your biggest total for income over the entire quarter.

Part 2. Totaling Operating Expenses

1. Gather information about your expenses. Having meticulous business records is perhaps the most important key to ensuring that you have an accurate profit and loss statement. You can't account for expenses if you don't have them in your records.

- You'll need records for expenses your business has incurred during the time period you've chosen for the profit and loss statement to cover.

- While you probably will have no trouble accounting for major expenses such as lease payments or utilities, don't forget incidental expenses such as small supply purchases or temporary contract labor.
- If you purchase raw materials to create another product that you sell, those raw materials also are part of your expenses.
- Likewise, inventory for retail stores also should be included in your expenses for the purposes of a profit and loss statement.

2. Create general categories for operating expenses. How you categorize your operating expenses will depend to some extent on whether your profit and loss statement will be used internally or is being prepared for a third party, such as a potential lender.

- If you're preparing a profit and loss statement for a third party, you probably don't want them to have explicit details about your business and the expenses of your operation.
- For this reason, you typically want to use general categories such as "advertising" or "office expenses."
- On the other hand, if you're creating a profit and loss statement for internal analysis, you may want to itemize your expenses to a greater extent.
- For example, if you were experimenting with different methods of advertising and marketing, and you want to analyze how your business's income changed under each method, you might separate those out, having separate categories for internet advertising and television advertising.

3. Include non-operating expenses. Non-operating expenses essentially are any expenses incurred by your business that don't directly relate to the operation of your business, such as interest on existing loans.

- Non-operating expenses also include any legal or accounting fees and bank service charges.
- You can categorize these separately, or you can simply list them as "non-operating expenses" and provide the total for each period.

4. List any losses your business has incurred. Losses typically include any damages your business has paid out as a result of a lawsuit, or capital losses from the sale of company assets, which don't fit under any expense category.

- Unlike your expenses, your losses should be itemized specifically. In most cases, these amounts are unlikely to recur, so it's important that they're accounted for specifically.

Part 3. Finding Net Income

1. Decide whether to use a template or create your own spreadsheet. You can download a template online to use for your profit and loss statement, or use one that comes with your spreadsheet application.

- However, creating your own spreadsheet can enable you to customize the information to suit your purposes in a more precise way.
- If you're preparing a profit and loss statement for a third party, such as a lender, they may want the information arranged in a certain way, or require that certain data be included.
- If you know the information you need to include, your spreadsheet should fit your data – not the other way around.

2. Create your rows and columns. If you've decided to create your own spreadsheet, organize it with your income and expense entries as the rows, and your time periods as the columns. Your data will go in the corresponding cells.

- Your organization should make sense and be easy to follow. Typically, your income entries will cover the top lines of your spreadsheet, while your expenses will appear in the lines below.
- This flows naturally, since you will be subtracting the expenses from your income to find your net profit.
- Your first column will identify the types of income and expenses that appear in each cell of the table, and each column that follows will indicate the time period for which those numbers apply.
- For example, if your profit and loss statement covers a single quarter, your spreadsheet would have at least four columns – one for labels, and the other three for each month included in the quarter.
- You may also want to have another column to the far right for totals.

3. Decide which method you want to use to list your entries. There are two methods you can use in a profit and loss statement. The simpler of the two is the single-step method, through which you simply subtract all expenses and losses from all revenue and gains.

- Using the multiple-part method, you'll separate your operating income and expenses from other income and expenses. Your sales minus your selling and administrative expenses is your net operating profit.

- Adding your other income minus other expenses to your net operating profit gives you your net profit before taxes.
- The multiple-part method makes more sense if you have an inventory-based business such as a retail store.
- If you're preparing the profit and loss statement for a third party, they may dictate the method you should use and the figures you'll need. For example, many banks require profit and loss statements using the multiple-part method if you're applying for a small business loan.

4. Enter the applicable values. Once your spreadsheet is set up, you're ready to enter the figures you found for your income and expenses down each category during the time period. This also is a good time to double-check your math.

- You can set up your spreadsheet to total particular cells as you go, so your totals for each category of income or expense is automatically populated.
- Once you've entered all your numbers, you'll need to total your income for the entire period, and your expenses for the entire period.
- If you're using the multiple-part method, you'll need separate totals for operating and non-operating income, as well as for operating and non-operating expenses.

5. Subtract your expenses from your revenue. If you're using the single-step method, once you've entered all the numbers you have some simple math to find your business's net profit. The multiple-step math is just as simple, but involves finding operating profit first, then net profit before taxes.

- While the goal of a profit and loss statement, also called an income statement, is to find your net profit, this isn't the only figure of importance in the document as a whole.
- Your profit and loss statement provides a snapshot of the money coming in and out of your business during the time period it covers. You can use it to analyze your business's financial health.
- Seeing the raw numbers in spreadsheet format can help you identify areas for improvement, or evaluate experiments you made with different methods of operations.

How to Review a Financial Statement

Steps

1. Use the balance sheet to review the financial condition of a business, as of a given period, by looking at how it manages its Asset, Liabilities and Equity. Basic Equation of a Balance Sheet: Asset = Liability + Equity

- Asset = Remember that asset adds worth to a business. You look at how well it manages its asset by checking the financial value allocated to cash, receivables, short-term and long-term investments, inventory, fixed assets, furniture and fixtures, land and building. By doing so, you can determine if a business is able to sustain and grow operation or it will close down.
- Liability = Take note that liability consists all the outstanding loan obligations of a business. Obtaining loans is one of the ways to generate capital to support a business operation. Liability account will enable you to look at the balances of the accounts payables, bills payables, notes payables and all other payables. Most often, depending on a given situation, when you see that a business have high amount of liability, it may be a sign of trouble and inability to sustain its operation.
- Equity = Equity meant to be the capital of a business. It is the major source of money to support and sustain a business operation. When you look at the equity account, check the number of stocks, common and preferred, that were issued. In the equity account, you

will be able to see the real value of a business in terms of ownership . When you see a high equity balance, it can be a good indicator that the business is able to sustain and grow. The opposite means it is in trouble of closing down its operation.

2. Review the income statement report to understand the overall performance, profit or loss, of a business in a given period. Basically, it comprises of the following:

- Revenue = This account will show you the amount of sales derived in a given period. It may come from the service fees or sales price of goods sold, depending on the type of business being run. Take note that when a business have a high amount of revenue, it indicates good marketing and sales process that resulted to high sales volume of product or service. However, beware for it doesn't necessarily mean the business is profitable.
- Expenses = Signify the amount of cost to produce an item sold. It includes cost of the materials used, cost of the service rendered, interest expense, depreciation, bad debts expenses, etc. When you verify expenses account, you can check if the business is spending on improving its product, investing a lot of money on marketing (like advertisement), gives high salary and benefits to employee, or just plainly wasting money.
- Profit(Loss) Before Tax = Remember that revenue alone doesn't necessarily means the business is profitable. Because of the expense account, even if the business has high revenue, if it spends just the same level, it wouldn't be as profitable as it should be. Here are the guidelines to know if a business is profitable or not: Profit means the amount of sales was higher than the amount of cost to produce (Revenue > Expense). When there's profit, it means the operation of the business was doing good. On the other hand, Loss means the amount of sales was lower than the cost to produce (Revenue < Expense). When there's loss, it means the operation of the business was doing bad.
- Income Tax = the amount of obligation the business have to pay to the government. In determining the income tax, check the country in which the business operates because Income tax is derived by the tax rate given by a particular country multiplied against the Profit Before Tax.
- Profit(Loss) After Tax = Finally, once you determined the income tax to be paid, you'll be able to compute for the real amount of profit or loss after deducting the applicable amount of tax.

3. Use the Cash Flow Statement to understand the movement of cash in a given period. There are two types of Cash Flow Statement, an indirect method and direct method.

- Direct Method = presents you a condensed cash receipts and cash disbursements statement.
- Indirect Method = presents you cash movements by adjusting net income for items that affected reported net income but didn't affected cash.

4. Check the Statement of Stockholder's Equity to get the details on the movement of the equity account discussed in the balance sheet above. You will be able to verify in detail the total ownership of a business, like how many stocks it is allowed to issue and how many it was actually able to sell. The movement you will see in this report includes, common stock, preferred stocks, additional paid-in capital, and retained earnings.

5. Look at the Notes to the Financial Statement to read the narrative explanation of the whole financial statement. It will explain to you the standards that were used to measure each account in

the previous four financial statements, the balance sheet, income statement, cash flow statement and stockholder's equity. Also, you will be able to check the future plans and operations of a business.

Single-entry Bookkeeping

Single-entry bookkeeping is a method for recording your business's finances. You record one entry for every transaction. The single-entry method is the foundation of cash-basis accounting.

With the single-entry system of bookkeeping, you mostly record cash disbursements and cash receipts. You will record incoming and outgoing money in the cash book. Usually, you track assets and liabilities separately.

Cash Book

Record transactions with the single-entry system in a cash book. A cash book is a larger version of a check register. It uses columns to organize different uses of cash for your business.

Cash book columns track key information about your finances. Each transaction gets a line in the cash book. Record the following items with the single-entry bookkeeping system:

- Date: The day the transaction takes place
- Description: A brief explanation of the transaction
- Income/expenses: The value of the transaction
- Balance: The running total of how much cash you have on hand

The first entry in the cash book should be the cash balance at the beginning of the accounting period. During the period, record transactions as individual line items. The last line in the cash book should be the cash balance at the end of the accounting period.

The items in your cash book will vary, depending on your business. Here is a single-entry bookkeeping example for using a cash book:

Description	Date	Notes	Expense (Debit)	Income (Credit)	Account Balance
Starting Balance	6/1				2,000
Rent	6/3		800		1,200
Sales	6/8			500	1,700
Supplies	6/20		200		1,500
Ending Balance	6/30				1,500

Income Statement for Single-entry Bookkeeping

The single-entry bookkeeping system is centered on the results in your company's income statement. The income statement shows information about a specific accounting period. It is also called a profit and loss statement for small business.

The income statement shows profitability during a time frame. It begins with sales and itemizes financial details down to the net income. Sales and gains are at the top of the income statement. Business expenses and losses are listed next. The bottom figure is the net income, or the take-home earnings after expenses and debts are paid.

To create an income statement, compile information from your cash book. Take a look at the following profit and loss statement example:

Profit & Loss Statement

Start Date*	End Date*	Accounting Basis*	
1/1/2017	2/28/2017	Cash	Run Report

INCOME	
Product Sales	$9,315.00
Service Revenue	$5,000.00
TOTAL INCOME	**$14,315.00**
EXPENSES	
Job Supplies & Materials	$300.00
Misc. Expense	$2,015.00
Payroll Expense	$5,000.00
TOTAL EXPENSES	**$7,315.00**
NET PROFIT	**$7,000.00**

Difference between Single-entry and Double-entry System of Bookkeeping

If you don't use the single-entry method, record transactions with double-entry bookkeeping. The double-entry method is more complicated than single-entry, and it is the basis of accrual accounting.

With double-entry bookkeeping, you record two entries for every business transaction. Each entry is either a debit or credit. The entries are equal but opposite. Your debit and credit entries must be the same values.

Some accounts are increased by debits and decreased by credits. Other accounts are increased by credits and decreased by debits. The following chart shows how each account is affected by debits and credits:

ACCOUNT	INCREASED BY	DECREASED BY
Assets	Debit	Credit
Expenses	Debit	Credit
Liabilities	Credit	Debit
Equity	Credit	Debit
Revenue	Credit	Debit

Though double-entry is more difficult than the single-entry system of bookkeeping, the method offers benefits to small business owners. It reduces the chance of making an error because you must balance the entries. Some businesses are required to use double-entry bookkeeping.

Persons who use Single-entry Bookkeeping

Single-entry bookkeeping is the simplest way to organize your accounting records. But, the method is not the best fit for some businesses. Think about your business's size, industry, and specific needs before choosing a method.

Consider the single-entry method if you:

- Make less than $5 million in annual gross sales or have less than $1 million in gross receipts for inventory sales, according to the IRS
- Are a small business that operates as a sole proprietorship, partnership, S Corp, or LLC
- Collect customer payments at the point of sale
- Operate a service business

Consider the double-entry method if you:

- Make more than $5 million in annual gross sales or have more than $1 million in gross receipts for inventory sales
- Operate as a corporation or a partnership with a C Corp partner
- Send invoices or let customers buy on credit
- Have inventory

Single-entry bookkeeping is great for new businesses. Companies with a low number of transactions and uncomplicated financial tracking needs also benefit from single-entry. And, using the single-entry method is a good way to start learning how to manage your books.

Keep in mind that assets and liabilities are harder to track with single-entry bookkeeping. It's also easier to make common accounting errors because there is no matching system, like with double-entry. Single-entry bookkeeping shows less information about your business's financial health.

How to Convert Single Entry into Double Entry

(1) Take up the Statement of Affairs at the end of the previous trading period and open all those accounts which have not already been opened. Generally, under the Single Entry System, cash, bank and personal accounts are maintained. Now, it will be necessary to open/the remaining accounts and debit or credit them with the opening balances as the case may be.

(2) From the debit side of the Cash Account, accounts other than the bank account and accounts of customers (on the presumption that such accounts are already maintained) should be credited. For example, if one finds that Rs 5,000 was received by sale of furniture, one should credit Furniture Account with Rs 5,000.

If an entry shows that Rs 4,500 was received from X, no further treatment will be necessary because the account of the customer would already be there and it must have been credited with the amount. A frequent item will be cash sales. Cash Sales Account should be opened and credited with the amounts of case sales.

(3) From the credit side of the Cash Account, various accounts (other than the bank account and accounts of creditors) should be debited. On this side of the Cash Account, will be found amounts paid for cash purchases, for various expenses and for various assets acquired. All these accounts will be debited.

(4) Treatment similar to (2) and (3) above will be required for Bank Account. Cash paid in or cash drawn for office-use, payment made to suppliers by cheques or receipts from debtors will already have been entered in these accounts; hence, double entry will be required to be completed only in other accounts that may figure. For instance, one will know from Bank Account what bills have been discounted and what discounted bills have been dishonoured, or what the bank charges are.

(5) If a Petty Cash Book is maintained, the monthly analysis will have to be posted in the ledger—various accounts for expenses debited and the total credited to Petty Cash Account. The debit to the Petty Cash Account must already have been completed from the Cash or Bank Account.

(6) A complete analysis of the customers' accounts will have to be prepared. This will give vital information regarding credit sales, sales returns, discounts allowed, bills received, bills dishonoured, etc.

Suppose, the following are the Various Customers' Accounts

A

Dr.					*Cr.*
		₹			₹
Apr. 1	To Balance *b/d*	760		By Cash	1,240
	To Sales	3,480		By Discount	30
				By Bills Receivable	2,400
			Mar. 31	By Balance *c/d*	570
		4,240			4,240
Next year Apr. 1	To Balance *b/d*	570			

B

Dr.					*Cr.*
Apr. 1	To Balance *b/d*	600		By Cash	400
				By Bad Debts	200
		600			600

C

Dr.					*Cr.*
		₹			₹
Apr. 1	To Balance *b/d*	1,480		By Bills Receivable	1,480
	To Sales	3,750		By Cash	2,000
	To Bills Receivable—dishonoured	1,480		By Returns Inwards	200
				By Bank	1,500
	To Cash (Noting Charges)	20	Mar. 31	By Balance *c/d*	1,550
		6,730			6,730
Next year Apr. 1	To Balance *b/d*	1,550			

D

Dr.					*Cr.*
	To Sales	2,400		By Returns Inwards	200
				By Cash	2,100
				By Allowance for breakages	50
				By Discount	50
		2,400			2,400

E

Dr.					*Cr.*
	To Sales	4,560		By Cash	1,000
	To Freight	140		By Bills Receivable (two bills)	2,600
				By Cash	610
	To Bank (Bill dishonoured plus noting charges)	610	Mar. 31	By Balance *c/d*	1,100
		5,310			5,310
Next year Apr. 1	To Balance *b/d*	1.100			

Analysis

	Dr.					Cr.						
Name	Opg. Bal.	Sales	Charges	Bills Dishon-oured	Cash or Bank	Cash or Bank	Dis-count	Bills Recd.	Returns	Allow-ances	Bad Debts	Clg. Bal.
	₹	₹	₹	₹	₹	₹	₹	₹	₹	₹	₹	₹
A	760	3,480				1,240	30	2,400				570
B	600					400					200	
C	1,480	3,750		1,480	20	2,000		1,480	200			1,550
						1,500						
D		2,400				2,100	50		200	50		
E		4,560	140		610	1,000		2,600				
						610						1,100
Total	2,840	14,190	140	1,480	630	8,850	80	6,480	400	50	200	3,220

To complete double entry now, what is required is to:

(i) Credit Sales Account with Rs 14,190, Freight (or charges) Account with Rs 140 and Bills Receivable Account with Rs 1,480 and

(ii) Debit Discount Account with Rs 80, Bills Receivable Account with Rs 6,480, Returns Inwards Account with Rs 400, Allowances Account with Rs 50 and Bad Debts Account with Rs 200. No further entry is required regarding cash or bank, as this must already have been completed.

(7) A similar analysis of suppliers' accounts will reveal purchases made, bills payable dishonoured or other charges debited by the suppliers (from the credit side of the accounts) and discounts earned, returns outwards, bills issued to creditors, etc. (from the debit side of the accounts). Accounts other than those relating to cash paid or cheques issued will debit or credited, as the case may be.

(8) The proprietor will have to remember other items which require entries in the books. To take an example, if a piece of machinery has been disposed of, any loss or profit resulting from such disposal will have to be brought into the books.

(9) A trial balance should then be prepared to see that there is no arithmetical mistake.

CHAPTER 4

Skills for Becoming an Auditor

Some of the key skills required of an auditor include among others excellent problem-solving skills, a strong aptitude for mathematics, an understanding of finance, strong IT skills, interpersonal and communication skills, etc. An auditor should be able to examine financial control systems, analyze spreadsheet data, gauge financial risks, check records and reports for reliability, etc. Auditors consistently need to master or improve upon these core competencies for success in this domain. This chapter includes some vital topics such as performing a basic accounting audit, writing an audit report, preparing for a workers compensation audit, etc.

Auditor

An auditor is a person or a firm appointed by a company to execute an audit. Auditing is a complex career, involving many different job responsibilities:

- Auditing involves the review, analysis and evaluation of processes, products, services, systems, organizations and employees.
- Auditors assess the accuracy, validity, reliability, verifiability and timeliness of organizational information, as well as the sources and processes by which that information is produced. This is an important role, because management and external parties thereby obtain an accurate assessment of the organization under their stewardship.
- Auditors also inspect an organization's internal controls and the extent to which these controls manage an organization's risk exposures. Internal controls help prevent the theft of a company's assets and, if properly designed and executed, prevent data manipulation by employees.
- Auditors ensure that checks are in place to help with the effectiveness of financial and operational reporting. They also make sure that controls are in place to protect an organization's assets.

Constraints in resources (hiring internal or external auditors can be expensive) necessitate that an audit provide only reasonable assurance that statements are free from significant errors. Due to the high cost of audits and the fact that auditors cannot possibly verify every transaction that has taken place, auditors use statistical sampling and make a determination (with management) as to key focus areas. An audit is not a guarantee that financial statements provide a perfect snapshot representation of the organization, only a reasonable assurance that the statements are free of material misstatements.

Useful Personality Characteristics

There are a few personal characteristics that are important for an auditor to have:

Auditors should posses a strong ethical framework and report on issues (or anticipated issues) as they come across them. There is a temptation to "let things go" as further investigation may require more work or reveal embarrassing processes, performance and/or fraud.

Good communication skills allow auditors to have a rapport with a variety of employees, managers, directors and external parties. As auditors establish good rapport with a variety of individuals, however, they should keep in mind the objectives of the audit (for instance, the reliability, verifiability, accuracy and timeliness of information), as they can often be tempted to not report on issues discovered.

Strong interpersonal skills are important, due to the variety of informational requests - and often, resistance to those requests - required from a variety of sources. Strong and/or ambitious types may attempt to dissuade auditors from revealing embarrassing findings.

Auditors need to be team players. As the scope of the audit can be fairly large, it is beneficial to help in other areas of an audit when resource constraints warrant it.

Finally, "professional skepticism" is an important trait to have, especially when reviewing a company's internal controls. One needs to assess how perpetrators of fraud can beat a company's controls, and auditors need to design and implement a system that can effectively protect the organization's assets.

What Auditors Do for Companies

An audit may be executed on IT financial-reporting mechanisms, where auditors assess whether the numbers being processed and reported by the IT/accounting software are reliable, accurate and timely. If the accounting system has delays or errors in reporting product shipments or receipt of raw materials, for example, the income statement or balance sheet may be significantly distorted (if the transactions are large). Significant distortions mean that management may not be able to properly run the company, or investors may incorrectly value the organization.

In another case, auditors may ascertain a company's inventory-management system as well as its current inventory count. Obsolete inventory (which is essentially worthless) may still be on the books as regular finished-goods inventory, which overstates a company's assets on the balance sheet and provides a misleading picture for management and investors. Auditors will need to understand the root causes for the overstatement, and recommend periodic inventory accounts and/or security measures (depending on the cause) to management by way of an audit report. For instance, a supervisor may have to periodically sign off on inventory counts by junior personnel and apply a "common sense" test (i.e., Does this count seem accurate and reasonable?).

In another scenario, division managers may be making large refund payments to customers on a recurring basis (for a variety of reasons, such as volume discount programs, claims of damaged shipments, goodwill gesture, aggressive quarterly revenue management, etc.). In identifying risks of impropriety, auditors may recommend that the system automatically require a finance manager's approval for transfers over $50,000, for example, along with monthly reviews for transfers which exceed $100,000 per month for the division (the company may be a multinational corporation generating billions of dollars in revenues, and it may not be worth the managers' time to conduct transfer reviews of amounts falling below these thresholds).

Internal auditors are employees dedicated to assessing the company's internal controls. They can serve as full-time staff or temporary workers working to improve the efficiency and effectiveness of processes, find fraud and provide periodic assessment reports to management and the board of directors. Small organizations may not be able to afford having a year-round internal audit staff and may choose to outsource a portion (or all) of their auditing needs to external auditors. External auditors assess their clients' operational systems and financial statements based on agreed-upon project scope and engagement costs.

Which Aspects of a Company are Audited

Virtually any part of an organization can be subjected to an audit. Managers, the board and/or external parties can help to determine the priority areas based on their organization's unique circumstances. A helpful way to determine what is a priority is to determine the effects and amount of recurrence due to failed processes. Managers should generally focus on first fixing areas where this impact is high.

As a sample of areas on which audits can be conducted, consider the following:

- financial reporting
- information technology
- supply chain
- inventory management
- transfer-of-payment processes
- administrative procurement
- expense accounts
- revenue management
- employee performance
- environmental impact
- hiring practices
- internal controls
- tax and government compliance

Because of the large quantities of information and processes within an organization and the limited human resources with which to inspect and assess these at any given time, auditors often address only specific key areas as part of the audit scope. Stated differently, material and important data are usually addressed, while less significant areas are placed on hold. Auditors often use statistical sampling to help identify focus areas, and also evaluate processes based on tests. For instance, controls on an IT system designed to prevent unauthorized access to petty cash balances on a bank account can be checked by testing the software system.

How to Become an Auditor

Part 1. Earning an Education in Auditing

1. Take relevant high school courses. If you're interested in pursuing a career as an auditor, it may be helpful to take relevant courses in high school. This can help prepare you for future college-level course work, and may also help you determine if auditing is, in fact, something you want to make a career out of. Relevant courses that may be offered in high school include:

- Accounting
- Advanced mathematics coursework
- Economics
- Finance

2. Apply to college. In order to become an auditor, you'll need a college education. Most companies and organizations require at least a bachelor's degree, while some prefer applicants who have gone on to earn a master's degree. Some employers will hire graduates who hold an associate's degree, but these candidates must have extensive bookkeeping and accounting experience. Candidates who hold an associate's degree are typically hired as junior accountants, and must work their way up to more advanced accounting or auditing positions. Typically, though, to pursue a career as an auditor, you will need a bachelor's degree.

- Many auditors major in accounting or a related field. However, some colleges offer highly-specialized majors like internal auditing for prospective auditors.

- If you cannot find a college program in auditing, pursue a bachelor's degree in accounting, finance, or economics.

3. Participate in an internship. Internships are not required, but they provide great hands-on experience and may help you make connections in the industry. You can find internships by searching for auditor or accountant internships in your area, or by seeking out internship opportunities through specific employers like the Consumer Financial Protection Bureau.

- Consider doing an internship over the summer when you're not in school.

4. Graduate from college. Whether you intend to pursue a master's degree after graduation or directly enter the workforce, you'll need to do well in college and earn a bachelor's degree. Most bachelor's degrees can be earned in four years or fewer, while some programs may offer a joint bachelor's and master's degree that can be earned in a five or six year period.

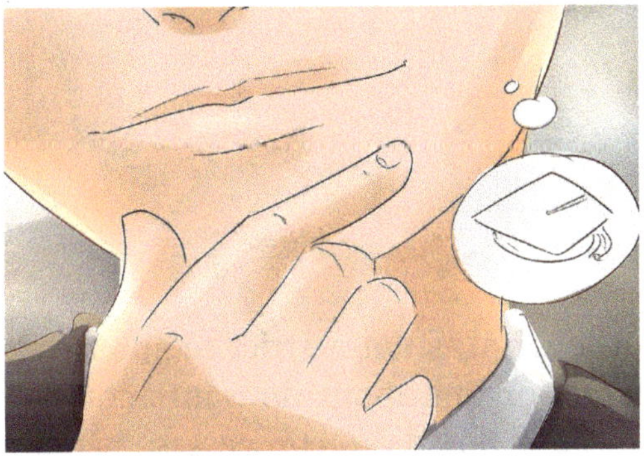

5. Consider earning a master's degree. Many companies do not require auditors to have a master's

degree. However, some larger firms may desire an auditor with a master's degree. If you decide to pursue a master's degree, you'll want to find a program that specializes in accounting, economics, or finance.

- If you want to advance your career in the field of auditing, then you will need to become certified as a CIA (Certified Internal Auditor) or CPA (Certified Public Accountant). To earn a CIA certification, you will need to have a combination of education and experience. To earn a CPA certification, you will need 150 semester hours of coursework, which is equivalent to a 5-year accounting degree.

6. Try to learn a second language. It's not necessarily a requirement at all firms, but learning a second language will help set you apart from other auditors in the job market. If you decide you want to work for a government agency or work in an area that has a lot of bilingual speakers, learning a second language may actually be a requirement.

- When choosing a second language to learn, focus on what would be most pragmatic for your field and your location. For example, if you plan to work in southern California, New Mexico, or Texas, being able to speak Spanish would be a valuable asset for most financial firms. If you want to work in a state in the northeastern United States, knowing French may be beneficial due to the close proximity to the Canadian border.

Part 2. Getting Certified

1. Consider getting certified. Though it is not a strict requirement to have certification prior to becoming an auditor, many larger organizations do want auditors who have certification. There are a number of different certification boards and processes, including Certified Public Accountant (CPA), Certified Internal Auditor (CIA), Certified Information Systems Auditor (CISA), Certified Government Auditing Professional (CGAP), and Certified Fraud Examiner (CFE).

- Of all the types of certification, the CPA is generally considered the most credible and desirable for auditors to have. That credibility is important, given that auditors work with employees, managers, executives, and members of the board, as well as external agencies and representatives.
- CPAs tend to make up to 10 percent more than non-CPAs, and typically have more job security.
- Be aware that almost all states require CPAs to engage in some form of continuing education (called Continuing Professional Education) to maintain the CPA license. Most states follow the CPE standards of the National Association of State Boards of Accountancy (NASBA) and the American Institute of Certified Public Accountants (AICPA), which is to earn 40 hours of CPE per year.

2. Ensure that you qualify. The National Association of State Boards of Accountancy (NASBA) offers an Advisory Evaluation to ensure that all prospective candidates qualify to take the Uniform CPA Examination. The Advisory Evaluation determines whether a prospective candidate has sufficient educational preparation for the Uniform CPA Examination and provides guidance on areas of study that the candidate may need to improve prior to taking the Exam. The Advisory Evaluation is important, as each state has its own specific requirements, including requirements that govern a candidate's education level.

- After passing the exam, some states mandate a minimum of one year of public accounting work experience before the CPA license will be granted. Other states permit different types of work experience to stand in for the minimum requirement.
- Candidates who earned an education in the United States must submit a $100 fee and an official copy of all college transcripts for the Advisory Evaluation. Not all NASBA jurisdictions offer the Advisory Evaluation. It is primarily offered in Colorado, Delaware, Georgia, Indiana, Louisiana, Massachusetts, Michigan, Missouri, Nebraska, New Hampshire, Pennsylvania, Puerto Rico, Utah, and Washington. If you do not live in a corresponding jurisdiction, you must contact the Board of Accountancy in your home state to determine where you can have the Advisory Evaluation performed. Keep in mind that Advisory Evaluation is optional. Check your state's requirements for obtaining a CPA license to determine if you need to do this.
- Candidates who earned an education through an international institution must submit a $200 fee and an official copy of all college transcripts for the Advisory Evaluation. Contact

your local Board of Accountancy to have the Advisory Evaluation performed. This report is used for professional examination and licensure by the Boards of Accountancy.

3. Understand the Exam structure. The exam consists of four separate sections: Auditing and Attestation (AUD), Financial Accounting and Reporting (FAR), Regulation (REG), and Business Environment and Concepts (BEC). The AUD and FAR sections take four hours each, and the REG and BEC sections take up to three hours each. Each section is graded on a scale from zero to 99, with a minimum score of 75 required in order to pass.

- Content and Skill Specification Outlines (CSOs/SSOs) address the content covered in each section of the Exam, and are available online at the American Institute of CPAs (AICPA) website.

4. Study for the Exam. The Exam is rather extensive in both the scope of material covered and the time it takes to prepare for and take the Exam. Most candidates spend approximately 500 hours total studying for the Uniform CPA Exam, though the total study time will, of course, vary from one person to another. Many candidates choose to take a CPA preparation class through local or national institutions, while others prefer to study alone. If you do study on your own, plan on studying for one to three hours every day for several months leading up to each section of the Exam. You may be eligible for a CPA prep class as an intern or new hire, and you may even receive bonus for passing the exam the first time you take it.

- The FAR section covers planning and reviewing, internal controls, obtaining and making records of information, and preparing communications between auditor/accountant and the organization. This section is generally considered the most difficult, and generally takes up to 180 hours of planning and studying to adequately prepare.
- The AUD section is difficult, but generally considered easier if taken after the FAR section. The AUD covers the standards of financial statements, the content required within a

financial statement, and how to account and report for a variety of different employers. It typically takes approximately 130 hours of planning and study time.

- The REG section addresses ethics and professional responsibility, business law, and tax and accounting procedures. It also takes approximately 130 hours of planning and study time.
- The BEC section is generally considered one of the easiest of the four sections. It addresses business structure, economic concepts, financial management, and information technology. The BEC is multiple-choice in format and takes upwards of 100 hours of planning and studying to prepare for the Exam.

5. Schedule and take the Exam. The Exam is administered by Prometric and is offered eight months out of the year: January and February, April and May, July and August, and October and November. It can be taken at one of over 300 test centers across the United States, and internationally in Bahrain, Brazil, Japan, Kuwait, Lebanon, and the United Arab Emirates.

- The AICPA recommends scheduling each test session a minimum of 45 days before the Exam.
- The NASBA charges a total of $729.08 to take all four sections of the Exam. There is also an initial application fee that applies to all first-time candidates, and that fee ranges from $30 to $200, depending on where the candidate resides and will be taking the Exam.
- The four sections of the Exam do not have to be taken at once. This would be exceedingly difficult, given the amount of preparation time required for each section. However, most states require candidates to take and successfully pass all remaining sections within 18 months of passing the first section.

6. Pay your annual dues. Having a membership with the American Institute of CPAs (AICPA) is

recommended, but it is optional. To maintain your membership, you must pay annual dues to the AICPA. The amount of a member's dues vary depending on the level of membership and the CPA's primary industry. For regular members, the dues requirements are as follows:

- Public accounting, law, and consulting partner/shareholder/owner/sole practitioner - $435
- Public accounting, law, and consulting staff - $245
- Business and industry president/CEO/COO/CFO/officer - $435
- Business and industry management/staff/internal auditor - $245
- Education faculty/administration - $245
- Government employee at the federal/state/local/international level - $245

7. Maintain continuing education requirements. If you've earned your CPA certification, you'll need to engage in Continuing Professional Education (CPE) every year. It is recommended that CPAs document all relevant CPE experience to keep track of their progress. The reporting period for having met the CPE requirements begins January 1 of each year.

- In most states, you will need to abide by the CPE requirements of the National Association of State Boards of Accountancy (NASBA) and the American Institute of Certified Public Accountants (AICPA). These requirements state that members must earn 120 hours (minimum of 20 hours per year) over a rolling three-year renewal period.
- College courses count towards CPE hours. The number of relevant CPE hours is determined by multiplying the number of semester hours by 15, or if the college uses the quarter system, multiplying the number of quarter hours by 10.
- A number of professional associations offer programs that count towards CPE hours. The number of relevant CPE hours is determined by multiplying the number of continuing education units taken through that association by 10.
- For programs that do not have a predetermined number of hours, the number of relevant CPE hours is determined by dividing the number of minutes actually spent in the program by 50.
- CPE hours are documented by keeping track of the class or program's sponsor, the title and description of the class/program's content, the dates and location of that class/program, and the number of CPE contact hours earned from that class or program.

- You will be required to submit all of your certificates and other documentation verifying that you have obtained the required 120 hours of CPE. You will also need to total these hours by category.

Part 3. Working as an Auditor

1. Embody the desired qualities. Though each firm's needs may be slightly different, there are some general skills and characteristics that are deemed desirable for auditors to have. Those qualities and skills include:

- strong personal and professional ethics
- A close attention to detail
- Analytical skills
- Communication skills
- Interpersonal skills
- Math skills
- Organizational skills
- Professional skepticism

2. Choose your desired industry. There are many industries in which an auditor may work. Auditors typically work alone in an office, though some work at home or on teams with other auditors and accountants. The primary industries auditors work in are, in descending order of employment percentages:

- Accounting, tax preparation, bookkeeping, and payroll services
- Finance and insurance
- Company or enterprise management
- Manufacturing

3. Write a strong resume. Prospective auditors looking for jobs will need to put together a strong resume. Some basic resume guidelines apply, such as using a standard 8.5 by 11 inch piece of paper with a simple, easy to read font (like Times New Roman). But there are some specific attributes that a prospective auditor should include in a resume. These include:

- Listing relevant coursework, including any classes that taught skills which were not derived from previous employment experience
- Showing quantifiable results from your past work experience - for example, detailing how much of an organization's operating budget did you control, how much overtime pay your cost-reducing initiatives saved, or how much (in percentage) company productivity increased after your employment
- Emphasizing how, specifically, your degree sets your education apart from other candidates' educational backgrounds
- Using relevant industry terms and phrases
- Detailing your achievements and accomplishments

4. Search for auditor jobs. There are many resources available online for an auditor seeking employment. In addition to traditional job websites like Indeed and Monster, there are a number of professional organizations for auditors that post job announcements online. The AICPA offers a

number of career resources through their website, including career opportunities at the AICPA and the Official Job Board of the AICPA.

5. Prepare for an interview. The financial world is much more fast-paced and driven than many other public sector jobs, and auditing is no exception. Many employers want to ensure that entry-level employees fresh out of school will be able to withstand the stressful work environment. To prepare for the interview, you should be well-versed in financial news and capable of handling stressful situations, all of which may be tested at some point during the pre-employment interview.

- Read financial publications, and be prepared to talk about those publications. Some experts recommend reading The Wall Street Journal and Financial Times to gain a general knowledge of current events and issues relevant to the financial industry.
- Brush up on financial concepts. The employer conducting the interview may quiz you on your knowledge of relevant concepts and your ability to make hypothetical decisions based on core concepts and financial models.
- Be prepared to prove your math skills during the interview. Not every employer will expect you to perform calculations during the interview, but it's not unheard of in the financial world.
- Ask your own thought-provoking questions. To do this, you may need to conduct a little research into the company's history, business model, and business practices. Don't ask "gotcha" questions, just form a sincere inquiry that will show that you've researched the company and have a genuine interest in learning more about it.

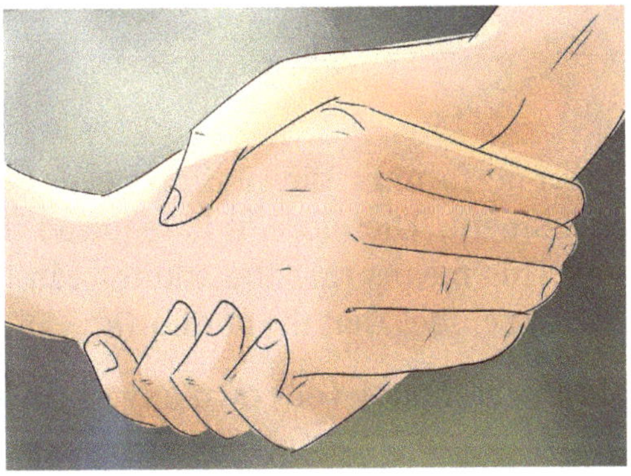

6. Make professional connections. Networking is an important part of any career, and auditing is no exception. As you build your resume and seek out new employment opportunities, it's

important that you remain aware of your professional network to grow and maintain your circle of connections.

- Expand your group of professional connections to include both superiors and inferiors. Your peers are a good start, but a diverse network of connections is important in any job search.
- Always carry business cards. You never know when you might meet a potential connection, including at social events.
- Be honest and upfront about what you're looking for professionally, and what you need your connections to do. If you need a recommendation, ask for one. If you need someone to set up an interview, see if anyone can help you with that.
- Always thank people for their time and assistance. Whether it's a prospective employer who granted you an interview, a former employer who gave you a glowing recommendation, or a professional contact who gave you a tip on an upcoming job announcement, always show your gratitude to everyone in your professional network. And any time you can, offer to help others out who are a part of your network.

How to Audit

Part 1. Planning the Audit

1. Confirm that you are suitable for performing the audit. It needs to be certain that any auditor is absolutely objective in their assessment. Therefore, it is required that the auditor be completely independent from the company. This means that the auditor can have no relationship with the company outside of the audit. This includes that the auditor(s):

- Not hold any interest in the company (not own any of the company's stock or bond offerings)
- Not work for the company in any other capacity.
- Be rotated regularly during the audit process to get fresh opinions on the material.

2. Assess the size of the audit. Before entering into the audit process, the auditor or auditing team should analyze the company and assess the scope of the work. This includes an estimate of how many team members should work on the audit and how long it will take. Additionally, it includes an assessment of any special or work-intensive investigations that must be made during the audit. Figuring this out can help the auditor assemble a team, if necessary, and can provide the company being audited with a timeframe for the process.

3. Identify potential mistakes. Before beginning the audit, the auditor should use their past experience and industry knowledge to attempt to predict areas where the company may have misstated financial information. This will require an in-depth knowledge of both the company and its current operating environment. Obviously, this is a very subjective assessment, so the auditor will have to rely on their own judgment.

4. Build an audit strategy. Once preliminary assessments have been made, you will need to create a plan to carry out the audit. Lay out all of the different actions that need to be taken, including

areas that you think may be of the most interest. Assign team members to each task, if applicable. Then, create a timeline for when each action needs to be completed. Know that this timeline may be changed significantly throughout the auditing process in response to new information.

Part 2. Conducting the Audit

1. Give advance notice. You will need to give the organization being audited plenty of time for them to get their records ready. Tell them the time period to be audited (the fiscal year, for example), and a list of documents that they need to have ready for review. These include:

- Bank statements for the year being audited
- Bank account reconciliation reports. This is where bank statements were compared to cash receipts and disbursements.
- Check register for the time period being audited
- Canceled checks
- A list of transactions that were posted to the general ledger (a manual or online system that tracks a company's transactions, including income and expenditures).
- Check request and reimbursement forms, including receipts and invoices for all expenditures
- Deposit receipts
- The annual budget and monthly treasurer reports

2. Verify that all outgoing checks were properly signed, accounted for and posted to the correct

accounts. If they can be substantiated, all the better. However, as an external auditor, that's not in your scope of influence. You just need to make sure everything was posted to the proper account.

- For example, there may be two different Accounts Payable, one for raw materials and one for office supplies.

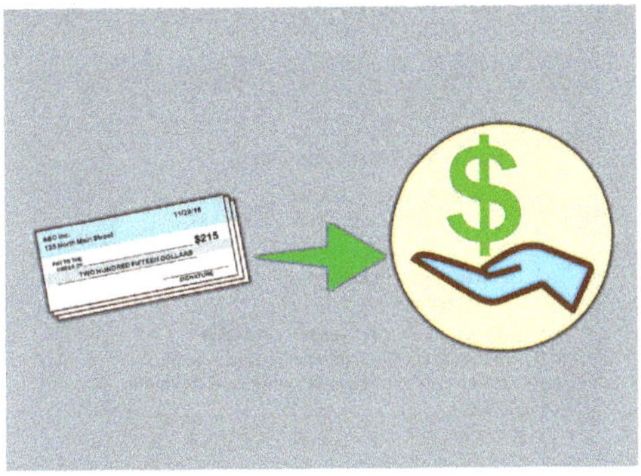

3. Ensure that all deposits were properly posted. This means they were entered into the correct accounts and ledger line in the general ledger. Very basically, these would be accounts receivables, but they should be further broken down (or could be) into specific receivables, depending upon the complexity of the organization.

- For example, revenue from the sale of a product would be entered into accounts receivable, while dividends issued might be entered into Retained Earnings.

Part 3. Auditing Financial Statements and Reports

1. Review all financial statements. These include balance sheets and income statements for the time period being audited. Ensure that all transactions are properly recorded and accounted for in the general ledger. Any unusual deposits or withdrawals must be noted and ensured that they were properly accounted for and legitimate. Check that all these accounts were reconciled monthly.

- An unusual deposit might be a very large amount or one from a business located outside the country. Unusual withdrawals would be if substantial amounts of money are going to one person or business over a long period of time.
- Reconciling means comparing two different reports or documentation. For example, cash and investments are compared to bank and brokerage firms' statements. Additionally, receivable and payable accounts should be compared to customer orders and bills,

respectively. For inventory, a physical count and valuation can be done at least once a year to make sure the information in the general ledger is accurate.

- For reconciliation, the auditor doesn't need to look at every single transaction. Taking a statistical sample of the total number of transactions (analyzing a small number and applying the percentage error to the whole set) can provide similar results in a shorter time.

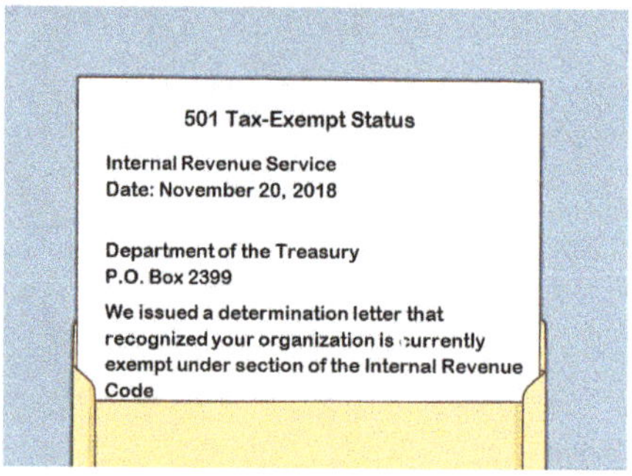

2. Ensure compliance with all state and federal requirements. If you are auditing a non-profit organization, verify their 501 tax-exempt status and that the proper forms have been filed. Ensure federal and state taxes returns, incorporation renewal and state sales tax forms, example, have been filed as necessary.

3. Review all the treasurer's reports. Make sure that what was reported was recorded and the totals from report to ledger books match accurately. Check to see that an annual treasurer's report was prepared and filed.

Part 4. Completing the Audit and Making Recommendations

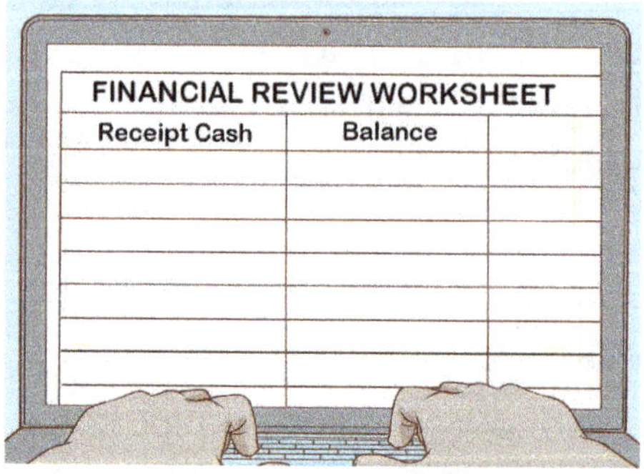

1. Complete the financial review worksheet. This is a summary of all the activity for the period

(usually annually, but could be quarterly as well). This includes:

- The cash balance at the beginning of the period
- All of the receipts during that time
- Any and all of the payouts during that time
- The cash at the end of the period

2. Suggest improvements to internal controls. Make sure to especially note when improprieties exist. If you are asked to do so, assess the organization's performance against their budget or other metrics.

- For example, you may want to suggest that two people sign every check, not just one. There may be documents that are disposed of at the end of the year, when they should be saved for a longer time period for tax purposes. Point out that originals need to be saved, not copies. Define the time period that all emails should be saved, usually for 7 years.

3. Determine your audit opinion. At the conclusion of the audit, the auditor must draft an audit opinion. This document states whether or not the financial information provided by the company is free of error and reported correctly under generally accepted accounting principle (GAAP) standards. Whether or not the reports meet these criteria is up to the judgment of the auditor. If they are reported correctly and free of error, the auditor issues a clean opinion. If not, the auditor issues a modified opinion. Modified opinions are also used if the auditor feels as though they were unable to issue a complete audit (for any reason).

4. Submit your signed document. This is a statement that you have completed the audit and you have found that either the ledgers are accurate or that there are issues. If you found any issues, such as missing checks or receipts (without explanation) or otherwise a math discrepancy, you should point those out in the report. It is also helpful to include any information you deem appropriate to assist in fixing those issues or preventing their recurrence for the next audit period.

How to Perform a Basic Accounting Audit

An accounting audit is the process of examining a company's entire financial situation, with an emphasis on ensuring compliance with relevant reporting standards, and promoting adequate cash handling policies and internal controls. In most countries, regular audits by outside firms are required for publicly traded corporations. In contrast, small businesses are typically not subject to as rigorous a set of reporting standards and controls and therefore are often not subject to mandatory audits. Learning how to perform a basic internal accounting audit on your own small business can provide you with a comprehensive understanding of your company's financial strengths and weaknesses.

Method 1. Preparing to Perform a Basic Financial Audit

1. Understand financial audits. Quite simply, financial audits exist to ensure that your business's financial information is "true and fair". For small businesses, the main concern is that all expenses and revenues are accurate so that the IRS knows exactly the financial status of the business and can confirm all deductions are valid.

- A formal audit involves an examination of financial statements by a qualified third-party (typically a chartered public accountant, or CPA). With regards to small businesses, audits are typically performed by the IRS due to concerns over proper reporting, whereas large public corporations typically hire external auditors (and have internal auditors) to confirm financial information is valid for shareholders.
- Despite this, you can still "self-audit" your business (or make sure your financial information and procedures are accurate and fair), to improve your business and protect yourself from an IRS audit.

2. Learn the reasons for a financial audit. There are several reasons and benefits to regularly audit your finances. While a basic audit can be performed by the business owner (who should be regularly making sure financial information is accurate and procedures are efficient), it is wise to hire a CPA to do a systematic overview of your finances.

- Financial audits can ensure information is valid and in accordance with accounting standards (like the Generally Accepted Accounting Principles, or GAAP).
- Financial audits make sure all legal and tax rules are being complied with, which can prevent an audit from the IRS, or different legal issues that can arise when fraudulent or incorrect information is presented to the public or investors.
- They can also provide education to the business owner about how their business is running and how it can be improved.

3. Prevent your small business from triggering an IRS audit. A basic accounting audit of your business can be an effective way to prevent yourself from receiving an IRS audit, which can be stressful

and time consuming. Before looking deeper into your finances, there are several initial tips that can be used to improve your financial standing and prevent an IRS audit.

- Ensure your deductions are realistic and not excessive (especially for business meals, travel, and entertainment). For example, daily commuting to work at a regular job is not a valid deduction, nor is claiming any personal expense as a business deduction. A good rule is if the spending is required to make money, then it can be deducted.
- Be sure you have proper receipts and records for any and all deductions.
- Have explanations and proper documentation for any major discrepancies between years. If you contribute much more to charity one year than another, include an explanation as to why when you file your return, and include any receipts or other associated documents.

Method 2. Creating an Accounting Audit Trail

1. Determine whether your business has a sufficient accounting audit trail. An accounting audit trail consists of the paper and electronic sources that document the history of a business's transactions. Audit trails are used to trace a business's financial data from the general ledger to the source of the transaction/funds. A strong audit trail provides a comprehensive chronological list documenting the steps taken to commence and complete transactions.

- Determine if your existing accounting practices enable you to track the complete process of a financial transaction with documentation. If not, your accounting processes must be strengthened in order to create a sufficient accounting audit trail. For example, if you are purchasing goods from a supplier, locate the documentation associated with the transaction (like an invoice), locate the transaction in the appropriate account (like the expense or accounts payable account), and identify what kind of transaction it was (buying goods from a supplier).
- Employ accounting software to create an electronic accounting audit trail for your business. Using accounting software to log your business's financial activities will allow you to easily store and analyze accounting data with ease.

2. Review your small business's existing record keeping policies. All financial information should be stored reliably, securely, and in an organized manner. All relevant information, such as bank statements, cancelled checks, and cash register tapes should be stored at least through the end of each reporting period. Having this information stored and readily accessible will help you resolve any issues or discrepancies that arise.

- There should be associated documentation for every transaction, with relevant explanations for transactions that will be used for deductions. For example, if you spent $100 on gas to travel to meet a potential client, there should not only be receipts (or bank records) for the transaction, but it should also be recorded that the $100 expense was to recruit a new client, and is therefore a deductible business expense.

3. Examine how financial documents are passed on to accounting personnel. The first step in your small business's accounting audit consists of gathering financial documents, such as invoices, receipts, and bank statements, and handing them off to the accountant or accounting department for processing. If this process is slow or unreliable, the accounting records will suffer and become unreliable.

- If you are self-employed, this step is simplified, and your task is instead to make sure that you take your own financial transaction records and process them quickly and regularly to ensure your records are up to date.

4. Create a system for monitoring your company's internal controls. Internal controls are those provisions that help to protect against fraud, theft, and other internal accounting issues. They are the procedures your business uses to ensure your assets are protected and your information is accurate.

- Separate accounting duties as much as is reasonable. For example, it is best not to allow the same person to both handle cash and do the bookkeeping, as this makes it easier to explain away missing cash.
- Safes should be locked when not in use, and company software and computers should be password protected.
- Camera systems are beneficial for monitoring the execution of internal controls at retail businesses.
- Reconciliation of accounts, such as the reconciliation of bank statements with the checkbook, should regularly occur as a way to validate financial information.
- Techniques like numbering documents such as checks to prevent duplication are also a useful internal control.

5. Consider the accounting and tax laws your business must follow. For tax purposes, you are typically required by law to keep comprehensive accounting records for your business. Preparing your accounting records to be in compliance with the law will make a potential federal revenue audit easier to comply with.

- Make IRS procedures such as keeping accounting records for at least six years a part of your internal audit trail process. This way you already have the processes in place that are required to respond external audits from the IRS and other external parties.

- To find out what laws are relevant to you, the Small Business Administration website is a very helpful resource. In addition, you can also consult with your accountant or bookkeeper if you have one.

Method 3. Conducting an Internal Accounting Audit

1. Employ industry-accepted audit practices. Good audit practices should serve as your initial guide for conducting your internal accounting audit. Using a business accounting software program, a tax attorney, or an accountant is the best way to ensure that your internal accounting audit is in line with generally accepted accounting practices.

- The General Accepted Auditing Standards (GAAS) are the most common auditing standards used to audit private companies. Consider the GAAS policies when commencing your internal accounting audit.
- GAAS are the basic rules and standards that are used when doing an audit. While these typically are used by professional auditors, consulting these basic principles can provide a helpful guideline for your own personal audit.

2. Cross-reference each part of your company's accounting system. Review each place into which accounting information is input, including the general journal, the general ledger, and individual account balances. Account balances should be examined on a continual basis, rather than just before preparing the trial balance at the end of the accounting period.

- Make sure that all entries have corresponding entries across each element of your system, and that any discrepancies are resolved quickly. For example, a purchase of merchandise to sell would require an debit entry to the inventory account, and a credit to your cash account.

- Use accounting documentation to verify your business's gross income, expenses and costs.
- If you have a very large number of transactions, it is acceptable to take a statistical sample in order to examine individual transactions, rather than trying to examine all of them.

3. Compare internal accounting records against external records. Check the fidelity of your own bookkeeping by comparing it against external records. For example, you can compare purchase receipts from your suppliers against your own purchase records. Note that issues that arise through this process may be due to external errors, such as miscalculations by a supplier or customer.

- If you encounter any errors, it is important to firstly correct the error. Any errors on the behalf of external factors (like a supplier error), should also be corrected by contacting the party involved. Next, it is important to document the error, and ask yourself why the error happened, and who is responsible. Is it a one-time mistake, or is there a problem with basic policy or procedure? From here, you can focus on ensuring the error is not repeated.
- If you have physical products or use equipment in your business, you will need to conduct physical audits as well. For example, inventory or equipment should be counted and visually inspected.

4. Check internal tax records against your tax returns. Look through your recent government tax receipts and compare these against your internal records regarding taxes paid and tax liabilities. In the U.S., keep tax receipts on hand for at least 7 years, as this is the statute of limitations on tax fraud.

5. Create an audit report. Compile a list of your findings into a succinct audit report. An audit report is simply a document that summarizes the findings of your audit. It will state problems you found, improvements that were made, and areas that were working well.

Since this is your own audit, this does not need to be a formal document, and should simply be a useful document that you can refer to for your own usage, or that you can show the IRS in the event that your business is audited.

How to Become a Certified Internal Auditor

Part 1. Meeting Eligibility Requirements

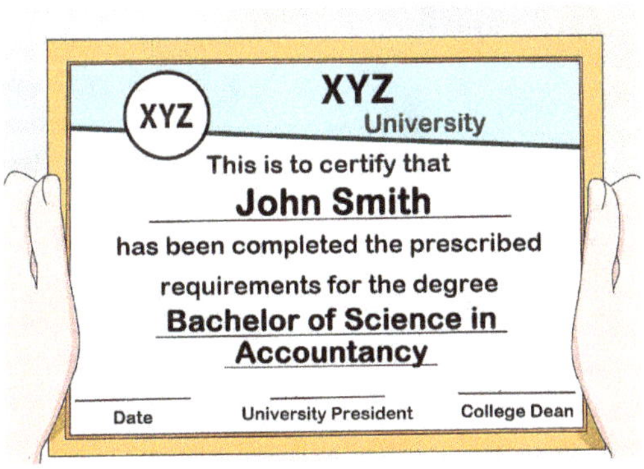

1. Earn a bachelor's degree in accounting or finance. If you haven't already earned an undergraduate degree, enroll in a program at a 4-year college or university. The most popular degree programs for internal auditors are accounting and finance. Internal auditors rarely gain employment without a college degree, and work experience is required in order to become certified.

- Beneficial courses include financial auditing, forensic accounting, business ethics, corporate management, and managerial finance.
- Information technology is a growing specialization among internal auditors. If you're interested in assessing a company's IT infrastructure and network security, you'll need additional coursework in computer science.

- A 4-year degree is not required in order to gain IIA certification, but keep in mind it's tough to get a job without one. The minimum education requirement is an associate's degree, but it must be accompanied by at least 5 years of professional experience.

2. Seize internship opportunities while you're in school. Your professors and school's career services office can help you find and secure internships. Interning with an accounting firm, government office, or corporate auditing department will offer invaluable professional experience and networking opportunities.

- Generally, auditing interns are assigned duties that are similar to any full-time employee. Tasks might include reviewing quarterly financial statements, verifying compliance with state and federal regulations, preparing reports, and identifying ways to improve clients' business efficiency and accounting procedures.
- During your internship, keep a log of your daily tasks and accomplishments. Do your best to talk to junior and senior auditors, managers, and other members of the team. Ask about their career paths, what interests them most about the field, and if they can offer any advice on career planning.
- Having at least 1 internship under your belt is crucial to gaining employment after college. Many entry-level auditors and accountants land their first job at a firm where they interned.

3. Pursue graduate studies for an advantage in the job market. While not required, consider obtaining a Master of Business Administration (MBA), master of finance (MFin), or master's degree in accounting. A graduate degree could give you an edge over competing job applicants, and it counts as a year of professional experience for the IIA CIA program.

- Master's degrees in accounting and finance usually take less time to complete than an MBA. An MBA is broader in scope, and could open the door to fields outside of financial auditing, such as executive leadership.
- The right choice also depends on your planned area of focus. An Master in Finance or accounting degree would be a good choice if you'll specialize in financial auditing. For specializations in administrative areas, such as operational efficiency and regulatory compliance, and MBA would offer a strong foundation.

4. Gain at least 1 to 2 years of professional experience. If you hold a bachelor's degree, you'll need at least 2 years of professional experience in order to become IIA-certified. You'll need at least 1 year of experience if you hold a graduate degree related to accounting, business, or finance.

- An entry-level auditor works with an accounting firm or internal auditing department under the supervision of senior auditors and an auditing manager. Search online for entry-level internal auditor, financial auditor, or night auditor postings.
- Keep in mind internships are a key step to landing your first job. Potential employers still need to see professional experience, even if you're applying for an entry-level position.
- Check for openings at the firm you interned for; even if there are none, send your resume and cover letter. In the cover letter, express your gratitude for everything you learned, and ask that they keep your resume on file and consider you for any future openings.
- If you can't get a job as an entry-level auditor, expand your search to include accounting and bookkeeping positions. If you don't have much practical experience, working in a company's accounting department could be a stepping stone to becoming an auditor.

Part 2. Filling out the CIA Program Application

1. Become an IIA member to save on exam fees. Join the IIA as a student or once you've landed your first entry-level auditing position. If you live in the United States, the annual fee for a professional membership is $255 (U.S); student members pay $40 per year. It's a worthy investment, as certification costs are $855 for professional members, $655 for student members, and $1315 for non-members.

- Become an IIA member at https://join.theiia.org.

- If you live outside of the U.S., membership dues vary by location. Find information about your nation's chapter at https://global.theiia.org/pages/institutes.aspx.
- It's wise to become a student member while you're still in college. The annual membership fee is only $40, it looks good on your resume, and you'll have access to career development resources, internship listings, and job postings.

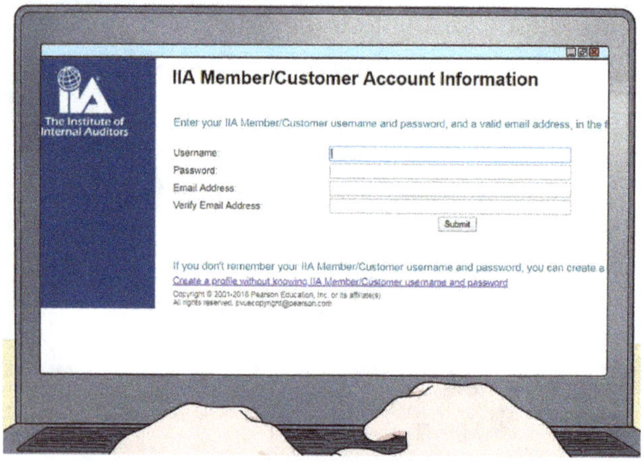

2. Create a profile in the Certification Candidate Management System (CCMS). The CCMS is an online portal through which you'll submit your application, upload your required documents, and pay your fees. To start your profile, click on "First Time Users," agree to the terms of use, then enter your name, email address, and contact information into the required fields.

- Create your CCMS profile at https://global.theiia.org/certification/enrolled/Pages/Access-CCMS.aspx. Click on the "Access CCMS" link to load the portal, then find "First Time Users" at the right side of the screen.

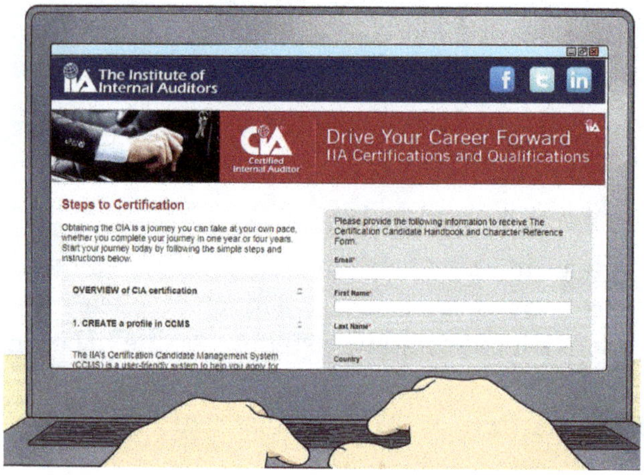

3. Complete your application form. On the CCMS main page, locate "Complete a Form," then click on the CIA program link. Enter your name, IIA membership number (if applicable), date of birth, contact information, and other details into the required fields.

- Fill out the digital form directly through the portal instead of filling out a printed paper copy.

4. Pay your application fee. You'll also need to submit your payment information on the application form. Acceptable payment forms include credit or debit, check, money order, or wire transfer. If you're paying by credit or debit, enter your card number and expiration date on the application form.

- If you're paying by check or wire transfer, check the appropriate box on the application form. Mail your check or money order to the address listed on the application form, or use the information on the form to direct your transfer.
- There's a $15 additional charge for wire transfer payments. For checks drawn from bank accounts outside the U.S., there's an additional charge of $30.
- Submit the completed application form through the CCMS portal after you've entered your payment information.

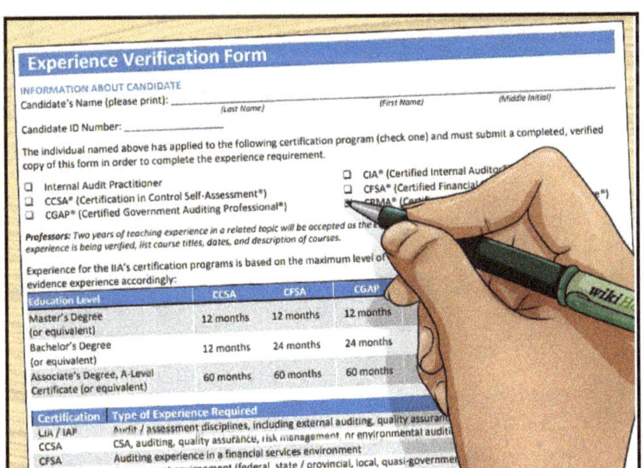

5. Fill out the experience verification form. Enter your name, job title, dates of employment, employer, and employer's contact information. If you've held multiple auditing positions, you'll need to submit a form for each job.

- Find the experience verification form at https://na.theiia.org/certification/Public%20 Documents/Experience_Verification_Form.pdf. You'll also see it in the CIA section of the CCMS.

6. Ask your supervisor or professor to be a character reference. Your reference will need to fill out a 1-page form affirming that you meet the ethical standards required to be an internal auditor. Have your reference fill out a digital copy of the character reference form, then upload it onto the CCMS portal.

- Download the character reference form at https://na.theiia.org/certification/Public%20 Documents/Character_Reference_Form.pdf.
- The form only entails entering names and contact information and adding a signature. Your reference won't need to write an additional letter.

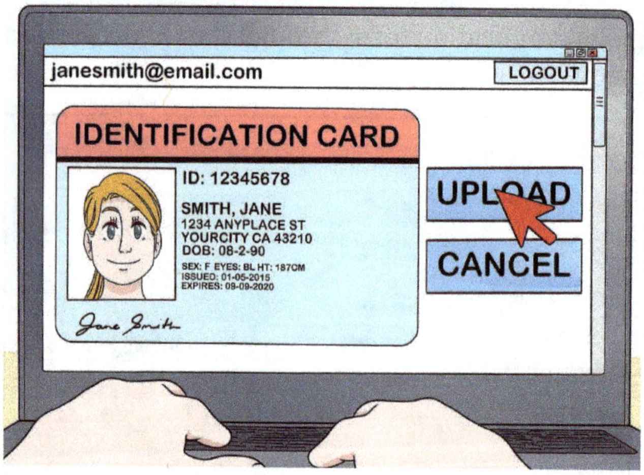

7. Upload your required documents. After submitting your application form, find the document upload link on the CCMS. Submit digital copies of your degree or official college transcripts, the character reference form, 1 or more experience verification forms, and proof of identity.

- Your proof of identity must be a scanned copy of your current (unexpired) passport or government-issued photo ID.
- You must upload your required forms within 90 days of submitting your CIA program application. If you don't upload your documents in that time frame, your application will be voided, and you'll forfeit your application fee.

Part 3. Taking the Certification Exam

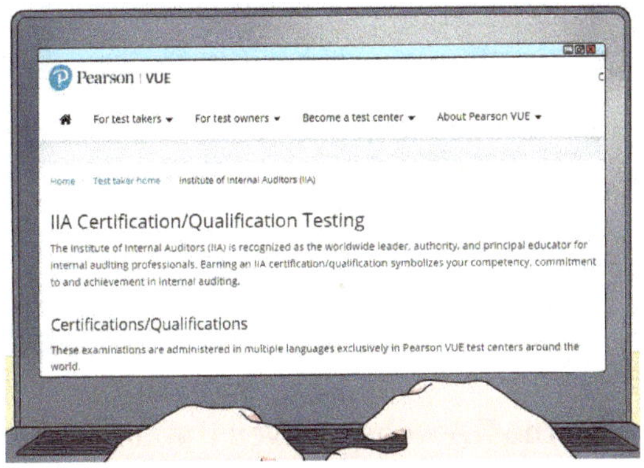

1. Register for the exam 48 hours after receiving your authorization email. After you've submitted your application and required documents, you'll receive an email that contains an authorization code. You'll be able to use the code to register for the exam 48 hours after the authorization email was sent.

- Typically, it takes around 5 business days for applications to be processed. All IIA exams are managed by Pearson VUE. Register for and schedule the 3 exam sections at https://home.pearsonvue.com/iia.
- You'll need to pay for each exam section when you register. Section 1 costs $280, and sections 2 and 3 cost $230 each.

2. Schedule the 3 parts within 180 days of each other. Schedule each exam section individually, and choose dates that are convenient for you. To ensure you have time to prepare, schedule the first section at least 2 to 3 months after you receive your authorization email. •After registering and scheduling an exam section, Pearson VUE will send you a confirmation email, which you should print and bring to the exam.

- You must take the first section within 180 days of your application's approval. You'll then need to take the next exam section within 180 days of the previous section, and the third within 180 days of the second.
- Part 1. of the exam takes 2.5 hours, and the other 2 sections each take 2 hours. Because they're so rigorous, taking the 3 sections on the same day is impractical.

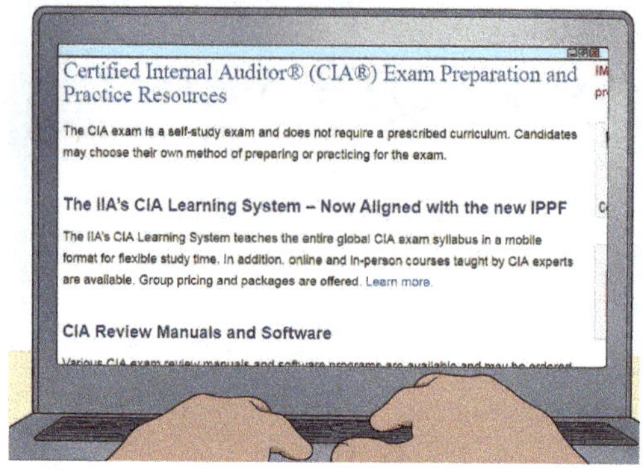

3. Access exam prep resources on the IIA website. Even if you're an experienced auditor, you'll still need to study for the IIA exam. With a 40% pass rate, it's a tough exam, but there are plenty of resources at your disposal. Take practice tests, check out the list of recommended reference books, and download IIA exam review courses.

- The test is comprised of multiple choice questions on 15 topics, including foundations of internal auditing, risk management, fraud risks, performing field work, information security, and information technology. Check the exam syllabus for the complete lists of topics and the reference texts that correspond with each topic.
- The first exam section covers topics 1 through 7, and the second and third sections each cover 4 topics. If you have 2 to 3 months to study for each section, you can focus on 1 topic per week, then spend at least 1 to 2 weeks taking timed practice tests for each section.
- Find the exam syllabus, practice exams, sample exam questions, tutorials, and other resources at https://global.theiia.org/certification/CIA-Certification/Pages/Exam-Preparation-Resources.aspx.
- You can also find IIA groups on Facebook and LinkedIn, where you can get in touch with people also studying for the exam.

4. Arrive to the testing center 30 minutes early. On testing day, bring your valid photo ID and printed copies of your IIA authorization email and the confirmation sent by Pearson VUE. Showing up 30 minutes early will ensure you have time for sign-in procedures.

- The test is computer-based, so you don't need a pencil or any other tools.

- You can't bring any personal items into the testing room, so leave your phone, watch, bags, and wallet in your car. If you won't be driving to the exam, call your testing center and verify that they have lockers or another secure storage space.

5. Retake an exam section within 90 to 180 days, if necessary. You'll receive an unofficial score immediately after taking an exam section and an adjusted score within a few days. If you received less than 70%, you may retake an exam section without paying any additional fees.

- You must retake the exam section within 90 to 180 days of the initial test date. You have 4 years to complete the CIA program, and you can retake exam sections without paying an additional fee during that time.

6. Order your certificate after passing all 3 exam sections. After you've passed each section, you'll receive an email informing you that you've successfully completed the CIA program. Congratulations. You can then head to the CCMS portal, and submit the certificate order form.

- After logging in to CCMS portal, scroll down to the section labeled "Certificates," then select "Certified Internal Auditor."
- On the form, you'll need to enter your Certificate Serial Number, which was included in the email notifying you that passed the program. You can also find this number on the "Certification Progress" section on your CCMS main page.
- The certificate and standard shipping are free. Expedited shipping is available for a surcharge. Additional copies of your certificate cost $50.

Part 4. Continuing Your Education

1. Complete at least 40 hours of continuing education per year. In order to maintain your certification, you'll need to participate in IIA-approved professional development activities. Acceptable examples of continuing education include courses on topics related to your field, seminars and conferences, and publishing academic work.

- Find continuing education opportunities at https://na.theiia.org/certification/certified/Pages/CPE-Opportunities.aspx.

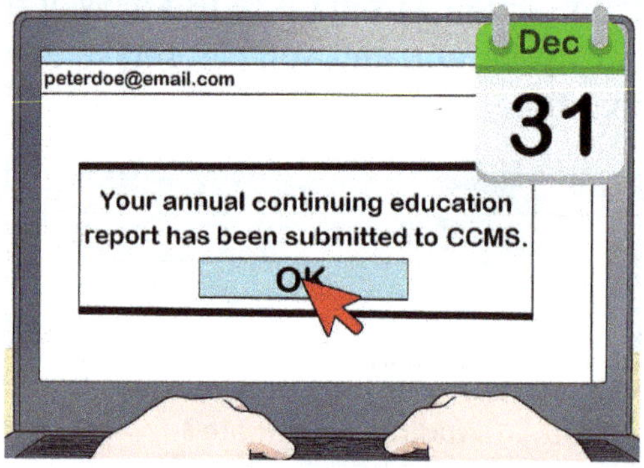

2. Report your annual continuing education hours by December 31. The reporting window opens in September; you'll receive an email by then reminding you to submit your hours. To report your continuing education hours, log into your CCMS profile, then head to the "Complete a Form" link.

- Find the reporting form for the current year, then enter your continuing educational activities and the hours you earned for each item.

3. Pay your reporting fee or annual membership fee. If you live in the U.S. and are an IIA member,

you don't need to pay anything to continue your CIA status. Fees vary if you live outside the U.S. and are an IIA member, so check with your national chapter.

- If you're a member, you'll need to pay your annual fee, which is $255 for professionals living in the U.S.
- If you're not a member, you'll need to pay a reporting fee of $120 to maintain your CIA status.

How to Write an Audit Report

An audit report is the formal opinion of audit findings. The audit report is the end result of an audit and can be used by the recipient person or organization as a tool for financial reporting, investing, altering operations, enforcing accountability, or making decisions. An effective audit report is essential to making sure the results of your audit are presented in a way that is useful to the party receiving the audit.

Part 1. Preparing to Write an Audit Report

1. Learn the different types of audit. An audit is considered an official examination to verify that proper policies and procedures were followed, and therefore, an audit can take many forms.

- Financial Audit: This is the most commonly known form of audit and refers to the systematic review of a company's financial reporting to ensure all information is valid and conforms to GAAP standards.
- Operational Audit: An operational audit is a review of an organization's usage of resources to ensure those resources are being utilized as efficiently and effectively as possible to accomplish the mission and goals of the organization.
- Compliance Audit: A compliance audit is performed to determine if an organization or program is operating in according with laws, policies, regulations, and procedures.
- Investigative Audit: These are typically commissioned when there is an assumed violation of rules, regulations, or laws, and may involve a blend of all the previously mentioned types of audit.

2. Understand the basic goals of all audit reports. Before delving into the specifics of writing an audit report, it is important to have a broad view of the major objectives of all audit reports. Having these in mind as you delve into the technicalities of writing a report will make sure your report does what it is supposed to do.

- Illustrating non-conformities: The main goal of any audit report is to illustrate where the organization does not conform with whatever standard, rule, regulation or objective that it is supposed to. It is important to clearly identify the non-conformity, as well as the standard it does not conform to. It is then important to demonstrate which evidence you used to confirm the non-conformity. The goal is that each non-conformity will contain enough information so that the receivers of the audit report can change it.
- Outlining positives: An audit report should not just include negatives. This is especially true for compliance reports, and operational audits. This allows the organization to focus on areas that are working and apply these to other areas. For example, if you are conducting a compliance audit to ensure an organization meets training requirements, you may say, "The audit reveals the current training program has exceeded requirements on-time and on-budget".
- Opportunities for improvement: Beyond indicating things that are not conforming to requirements (non-conformities), it is important to also indicate high-risk areas, or areas that may be in compliance but are at risk of eventually not complying, or could be improved.

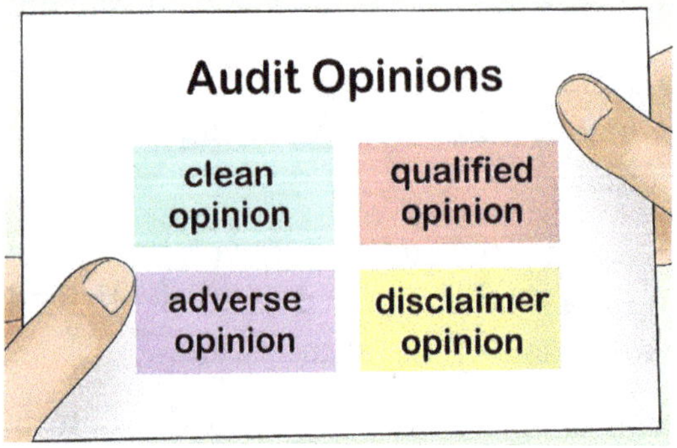

3. Learn the types of audit opinions. If you are writing a financial audit report, for example, it is important to understand there are four basic types of opinion that can be expressed. Which opinion you express affects the tone, structure, and organization of an audit report, and the type of opinion

you express is determined by the results of the audit. Other types of audits (like operational and legal audits) can use the same types of opinions.

- A clean opinion is used if an entity's financial statements are a clear representation of an entity's financial opinion.
- A qualified opinion is used when there were scope limitations on the auditor's work. Scope limitations are restrictions on the audit caused by the client or other events that do not allow the auditor to complete all aspects of his or her audit procedures.
- An adverse opinion is used if financial information was misstated.
- A disclaimer opinion can be triggered by several different situations. For example, the auditor may not be independent or there are concerns with the auditee.

4. Think about who will be reading the report. Who will be reading your report, and what is their scope of knowledge on the language you will use? An audit report is an official record of an audit project, so it will likely be returned to in later years for re-audits. Define all the terms and abbreviations you use, as the standard forms of communication have potential to change.

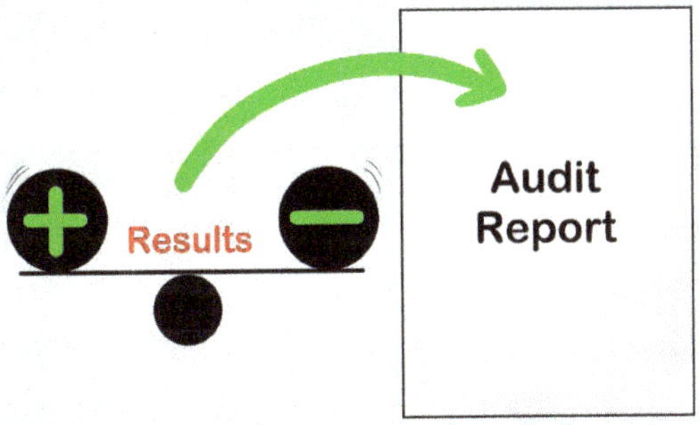

5. Know the style of audit reporting before you begin. There are certain style guidelines you need to follow for any audit report, so make sure you know what these principles are before you begin to write.

- Provide perspective for the reader, giving a fair balance of the positive and negative results of the audit.
- Be precise, and avoid redundant phrasing and inexact terminology. In interest of clarity,

opt for shorter sentences over longer ones. A limit of 15 to 18 words is recommended in business writing. Also, avoid intensifiers like clearly, special, key, and reasonable as these lack precision.

- Do not use passive voice. Passive voice can be difficult to read. Instead of saying "No irregularity of operation was found" say "The audit team found no evidence of irregularity."
- Use bullet points, which break up difficult information and make it clearer for the reader.
- Use gender neutral terms.
- Do not use audit buzzwords. Buzzwords are ambiguous, overused phrases like "generally improved," "significant risk," and "tighten controls."

6. Outline your audit report. Before you begin writing, read the results of the audit and make an outline for yourself based on all the sections you will need. A standard outline is comprised of headings, marked by Roman Numerals, and subsections that use letters, numbers, or lowercase Roman Numerals. Pick and organizational strategy that works for you and go from there.

- For example, if you are auditing the processes for a particular department of an organization, you may consider breaking the department up into several key sections and reporting findings that way.

7. Write your Introduction. The introduction overviews information about the audit area, and informs the reader of any background they might need to know before reading the full report.

8. Follow with the Purpose and Scope Methodology. This section provides information about the audit and should answer the following questions, as well address the methodology used in the audit:

- Why was the audit conducted?
- What was included and not included in the audit?
- What was the time period audited?
- What were the audit objectives?

9. Continue onto the Statement on Auditing Standards. This audit is a basic disclaimer people will look for to make sure the audit was conducted correctly. The Statement on Auditing Standards should say the report was conducted according to government standards.

10. Write the Executive Summary. This is an overview of the audit results. It should present overall

conclusions and recommendations related to the Purpose and Scope Methodology. This section must include:

- A brief description of what was audited, objectives, scopes, and time periods.
- Statements of significant action plans.
- Overall statements of concerns and conclusions.
- Overall audit report rating.

Part 2. Writing Your Results and Recommendations

1. Write an opening statement for your findings/recommendations section. An audit report typically ends with results from the audits and recommendations for improving the entity audited. Results and recommendations are the foundation of a good report. Before you begin writing this section, provide a brief opening statement that outlines the information you will be providing.

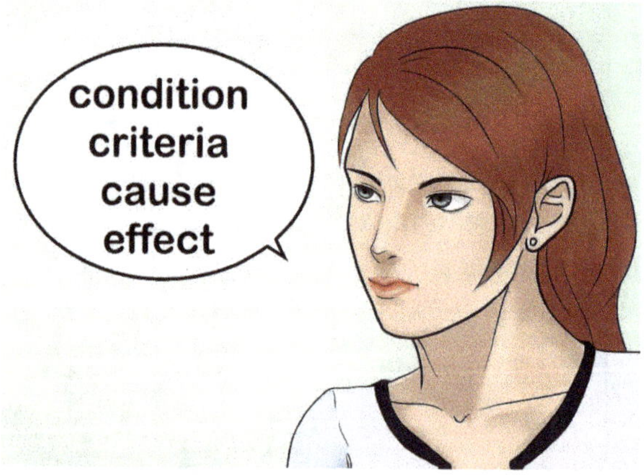

2. Understand condition, criteria, cause, and effect. The findings of your audit report are reliant on these terms, and understanding and addressing them in each finding is key to a good report.

- Criteria is an explanation of management goals and the standards use to evaluate the program, function, or activity audited.
- Condition is how effectively department management is meeting goals and/or achieving standards. Goals can either be fully achieved, partially achieved, or not achieved.

- Cause is a statement on the reason things have gone well or poorly. Possibilities include inadequate procedures, procedures not being followed, poor supervision, or unqualified employees.
- Effect states the result of the conditions, in quantifiable terms. Is the effect increased risk or exposure? Is it monetary cost? Is it poor performance? This should be addressed when you cover effect.

3 Make effective recommendations. As an auditor, your final task is making recommendations for improvement for the entity audited. They should be listed together under a lead statement such as "We recommend that the department director:" Remember to do the following while writing your recommendations:

- Be positive. Focus on what is going right at the moment, and how the good aspects of the entity can be applied in ineffective areas.
- Be specific. Be very clear as to what specific aspects do not adhere to protocol, and to what concrete steps could be potentially implemented to ensure compliance.
- Identify who should act. Does the company need better employee performance or should management be picking up the pace? Make clear who needs to make changes.
- Keep recommendations brief. Be succinct - only include details that are necessary to your point.

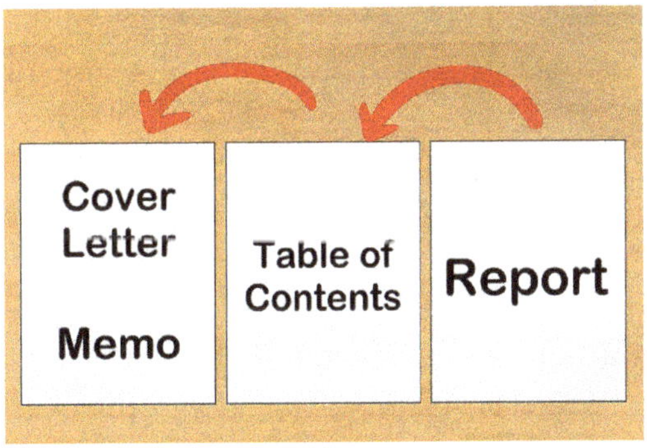

4. Follow proper format. When you are polishing up your audit report to send to management, make sure to follow proper format before you send it out. •Include a cover page. The cover page should be three or four lines, and outline the subject of the audit report and the type of audit.

- A memo should follow the cover page. The memo should be one or two short paragraphs overviewing who and what was audited, who has received or is receiving the report, and plans for future distribution.
- A table of contents follows the memo, and it contains a catalogue of chapters, page numbers, sections, and suggestions of the audit.
- The report should be written in plainly-worded, non-technical language and use proper grammar and paragraph organization.
- Reports are organized by chapters, each with a title, and by sections and subsections, each marked with a heading. Headings should go from general to more specific.

How to Become a Night Auditor

Night auditors work at the front desk at hotels, motels, inns and other types of lodges. Your job tasks will include checking in guests, taking reservations, and checking out guests. You'd also be responsible for accounting duties; you'd reconcile the daily ledger to accurately account for usage of rooms and the collection of money that pays for services. Although a college degree is not absolutely necessary to successfully enter this field, you should at least have some experience, particularly in accounting or bookkeeping.

Part 1. Getting the Appropriate Education and Experience

1. Gain a degree in hotel management. Ideally, you'll have an undergraduate degree for this job. Some hotels will hire you without one, but it puts you above the competition if you have that degree.

- You'll take courses like the basics of hotel management, event management, and food and sanitation.
- You can also get a business management degree with a focus in hospitality management.
- While working on your degree, choose a focus in auditing, if you know that's what you want to do. By focusing on auditing, you'll give yourself that much more of an edge.

2. Apply for an internship. One possibility to gain experience is to work as an intern. Some of the larger hotels and chains offer internship programs so you can get your feet wet. Keep in mind that it will likely not be a paid internship, though it may be paid in some cases. Even if it's not, you may be able to get course credit for it.

- Try asking around at your school for internship possibilities. Companies often contact schools to find interns.
- You can also check with some of the big hotels in your area to see if they offer internships.

3. Find an entry-level job at the front desk of a hotel. For some hotels, experience is even more important than a degree. The best experience is working in another job in the hotel. Take an entry-level position that's similar, such as providing support to the front desk. Any kind of bookkeeping experience is also helpful.

4. Improve your accounting skills. Part of being a night auditor is doing some basic accounting. For instance, you'll usually run the numbers for the day, as well make sure the accounts match up. You'll likely prepare reports that the day auditor can check over.

- If your accounting skills aren't great, make sure to take some accounting classes while you're in school. If you're already out, try taking some at a local community college.

5. Work on your people skills. You may think that night auditors work in a dark room all by themselves. In reality, most night auditors manage the front desk at night. That means you'll need to deal with any issues that come up at night, as well as check in customers arriving late. Because customers are more likely to be worn out at night, you'll need to have excellent people skills.

- Working in retail is a great way to develop people skills.

6. Brush up on your computer skills. Night auditors generally work on the computer a great deal, so your skills must be up to snuff. Try taking a computer class at a local community college if you need to learn the basics.

- Learning about accounting software would be a great addition to your skill set.

Part 2. Applying to be a Night Auditor

1. Search for jobs. You can use a basic job search engine such as Monster, Yahoo., or Indeed. However, you can also find these jobs by searching for them on the websites of major hotel chains.

- Use "night auditor" as your search term. You can also narrow it down by city.

2. Tailor your cover letter and resume. Like any job, it's best to customize your resume and cover letter to fit the position. You want to highlight skills and experience that will benefit the company if you're in this position. Go down the list of requirements, and make sure you hit each one of those in your cover letter.

- In addition, highlight experience on your resume that's relevant to the job.
- Keep in mind, most hotels are looking for people who are good in customer service. You'll also want to highlight any math and computer skills you have, as well as organizational skills.

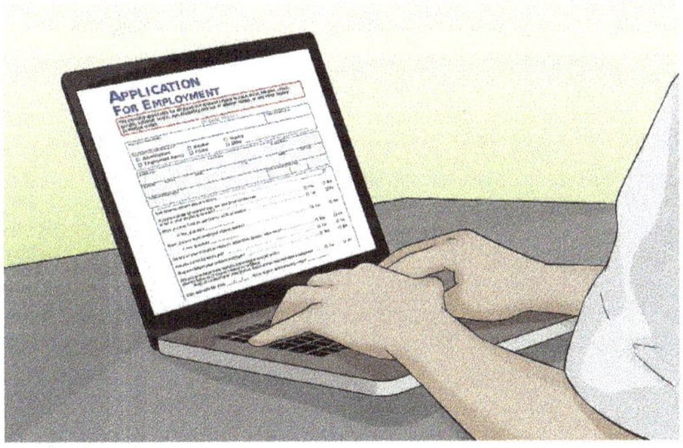

3. Send in your application online. Many jobs will allow you to apply online. You'll likely need to fill out an application form with biographical information, your work history, and references. Most places also require that you send in a resume and cover letter.

4. Visit hotels in the area. Another option for finding a job is to simply do the leg work. Go to a

variety of hotels, and ask if they are hiring night auditors. Make sure to have a resume in hand and dress as if you are interviewing that day, because there's an off chance that you might be.

5. Nail the interview by remaining calm. As a night auditor, you must do well under pressure, as you'll need to deal with emergencies from time to time. Prove you can remain calm by doing well at the interview; respond directly as possible to questions.

- If a question throws you, pause a moment before answering. Take a deep breath to clear your mind. If you need to, ask the interviewer to repeat the question.

Part 3. Starting the Job

1. Train for the job. Often, most of what you learn for this position will be done on the job. As a night auditor, you'll need to close out the transactions for the day. You'll also check people in and out, and deal with customer problems, as you'll likely be working the front desk, too.

- As your employer goes over the information, make sure to take notes, and don't be afraid to ask questions.

2. Get ready for the night shift. It seems obvious, but it's important to remember you'll be working at night for this job. Make sure that fits your temperament and that you'll be able to handle long hours by yourself. Before you start the job, try shifting your sleeping schedule back a little bit each night, so that you're more prepared for when you do start the job.

- It also helps to note on your resume why you want a night position.

3. Learn the emergency protocols. As a night shift person, you'll likely deal with more emergencies than the day shift does. Don't let the first fire alarm take you by surprise. Sit down and read any information provided about what to do in case of emergency, so you'll be ready.

- Night time lends itself to more "emergencies," mainly because people are in the hotel more at night. Plus, kids sometimes get bored. They may try to smoke in their rooms, for instance, and set off the smoke alarm.

How to Gather Audit Evidence

An auditor investigates a company's finances and operations to determine whether the company's records are accurate. In most cases, a CPA or certified auditor conducts an audit. If you are a business owner facing an audit, understanding how audit evidence is gathered can help you prepare for your upcoming audit. If you go through your records and company operations before the auditor arrives, the audit process may run more smoothly.

Method 1. Examining the Records

1. Review records for completeness: All spaces of a financial ledger or form should be filled in, and each entry should have a verifiable date. If any spaces are blank, there should be some notation or explanation as to why the information wasn't filled in.

- For records of meetings or interviews, the entry should include the action that was taken as a result and any other follow-up actions that were taken later.
- Include the names of anyone involved in an entry, and their role in the company, if applicable. For example, if you have a list of deposits made into an account, each entry should include the names of the managers or employees who made the deposit.

2. Compare account balances and transactions to banking records. Financial ledgers are attached to a business banking or investment account. The company's ledgers should reconcile against the bank's records.

- In some cases, further investigation may be required. For example, if the company's records note a $1,000 sale to a client, but only $500 was deposited into the company's account, the auditor might contact the client to find out how much money the client paid and when.

- Get recent bank statements and compare the company's records to the bank's records. If there is a discrepancy, mark the transaction and determine why the records are different. If you can identify the reason for the discrepancy in advance and correct your records if necessary, it will save the auditor some time and effort.

3. Test the effectiveness of internal financial controls. Inadequate controls leave room for error as well as an increased risk for theft or fraud. Make sure all financial software is up-to-date, and use complex passwords that are unique to each user. Make sure passwords aren't left lying around for anyone to use.

- The auditor will keep an eye out for any holes in the company's financial security that could be exploited. When information about these type of security risks show up in an auditor's report, it is an opportunity for the company to take steps to close those gaps to protect the company as well as its customers.

4. Reconcile debt computations with lenders. If your company is carrying debt, pull statements from the lenders and make sure the interest rates and principal owed match your company's books.

- The auditor will also evaluate who approved the debt, any mention of the debt in company meetings, and whether all debt payments are made in full and on time. Make sure these records are clear and available to the auditor.
- If the company leases work or office space, the auditor will also evaluate the lease agreements and make sure those obligations are being fulfilled according to the terms of the contract.

5. Recompute and evaluate expenses. Pull receipts, expense reports, and other expense records and determine their accuracy and legitimacy as business expenses. Unusual items or overly large transactions may be subject to additional scrutiny.

- For example, if a company usually has $800 in utility expenses each month, and one month the expense report notes $8,000 for utility expenses, the auditor would reach out to the utility companies for confirmation of the amount and determine why that month was excessive or if the amount was listed in error.

Method 2. Seeking Confirmations of Transactions

1. Send letters to customers and vendors for repeat transactions. For particularly large or out-of-the-ordinary transactions, write or call and confirm the amount and details of the transaction. Ask

the customer or vendor what their records say rather than simply reading your record and asking for confirmation.

- For example, if the company pays $2,500 to a particular vendor every month, and then in February the company's records show it paid that vendor $7,500, you could contact the vendor and ask what their records showed your company paid in February. If the amount is correct, ask for a detailed statement that could help you figure out why the bill was so high. If the amount is incorrect, adjust your books.

2. Verify supporting information for complex account balances. For some transactions, it makes more sense for the auditor to verify supporting information, such as rates, and then recalculate the total that should be there.

- For example, suppose there's a question about 401(k) withdrawals from employee paychecks. You can verify the rate of those withdrawals from employees, then recalculate the amounts that should have been withdrawn. Compare those calculations to the balances in the employees' 401(k) accounts.

3. Analyze market data to confirm financial statements. Particularly if the company trades securities on the open market, look at market data to determine whether your valuation in company financial statements is accurate.

- For example, if the company has invested in securities and plans to sell them in 2 years, you could analyze the prevailing market price and performance of those securities to determine their book value.

4. Check the terms of unusual transactions. Confusing or unusual transactions may raise flags for auditors, since they indicate a higher risk of fraudulent activity taking place at the company. Identify these transactions in your books and talk to customers or vendors to figure out what was going on.

- For example, a transaction for the purchase of a large amount of products, followed nearly immediately by a return of the proceeds of that sale to the customer without a return of product, might raise audit flags.

5. Use intermediaries for related-party transactions. If two managers, company officers, or employees are involved in a transaction, the auditor typically uses third-party records, if available, to confirm the transaction was above board. If you know those records exist, you can go ahead and request them to justify the transaction.

- The auditor will seek out audit evidence from any intermediaries, such as banks, agents, or attorneys, to confirm the business rationale and terms of the transaction.

Method 3. Inspecting the Premises

1. Verify the existence of assets through physical inventory. Something may be listed in the books, but that doesn't mean it's actually present. Particularly in a retail sales environment, regular inventory enables you to correct the books through the auditing process.

- Notes and photos, as well as inventory records, help document this evidence.
- Observe how broken or expired product is disposed of, and which employees have responsibility for marking down that product for the records.

2. Interview employees about policies and procedures. Employees may be questioned generally about policies and procedures, or asked specific questions about particular transactions that have raised red flags. While an employee interview on its own may not constitute objective, reliable audit evidence, it may point to other evidence or information.

- Employees in financial and managerial roles in particular should expect to have conversations with the auditor throughout the auditing process.

- In more serious situations, the auditor may submit written questions to employees so that their responses are preserved in writing.

3. Look for uncontrolled documents or nonconforming products. Random documents or notes posted on walls or machines may indicate an alternate procedure that doesn't exactly follow policy or that presents security concerns. The same is true for products that aren't kept or stored where they're supposed to be.

- For example, if an auditor of a retail store found piles of product hidden behind a desk in the office rather than out on the sales floor, they would want to determine the status of those products and why they were being segregated from the rest of the inventory.
- Notes taped to machines may indicate that something isn't working properly and needs to be repaired, or that staff members have not been properly trained on how to operate the machine. These random notes become a part of basic policy and procedure, even if their message isn't communicated through standard channels.

4. Note poor cleaning or improvised repairs. Walk through the workplace and look for machines or fixtures that have been temporarily "repaired" by employees using duct tape or shims. Implement proper maintenance procedures before the audit to make sure everything is clean and in working order.

- If a workplace is messy, it may indicate that there's a larger issue, or that a problem isn't being adequately addressed. This can raise red flags for auditors.
- Machines and fixtures are business assets that require regular maintenance to live out their service life. If these assets aren't being cleaned, repaired, and maintained properly, the company could lose money.

How to Become a Premium Audit Manager

Step 1: Earn a Bachelor's Degree

Though a degree is not always required, some employers prefer candidates with at least a bachelor's degree in accounting, insurance, or business administration. Educational programs in these areas teach fundamental principles and practices in financial management, business regulations, auditing, and tax law. To provide real-world application to the curricula, schools typically offer field work and internship programs that provide students with the chance to observe and work with experienced professionals.

Step 2: Get Experience in Insurance

In addition to relevant education, employers generally look for professionals with experience in auditing, insurance technology, and financial management. Working in insurance claims adjusting, policy sales, or accounting after college could help to establish a base of experience relevant to the field of premium auditing.

Step 3: Obtain Necessary Credentials

In some cases, employers request premium audit managers to be a Certified Public Accountant (CPA), Certified Internal Auditor (CIA), or Certified Financial Examiner (CFE). A state board of accountancy issues the CPA examination and requires supervised experience under a certified accountant prior to conferring the license, though the number of experience hours required varies. The Institute of Internal Auditors administers the exam for the CIA credential, as well as specialized credentials for controls, government, and financial services auditing. The Society of Financial Examiners allows experienced members who have completed at least one college-level course in management to test for the CFE designation.

Step 4: Acquire Optional Certification

Though professional certification is usually voluntary, a credential in premium auditing demonstrates specific knowledge of the field and can lead to career advancement. The Institutes, formerly the American Institute for Chartered Property Casualty Underwriters, offer an Associate in Premium Auditing (APA) program that prepares individuals for certification. Professionals can earn Associate in Premium Auditing (APA) and Certified Insurance Premium Auditor (CIPA) credentials by completing education and experience requirements, passing an 85-question exam, and submitting an essay on premium audit management.

Remember to complete continuing education. Licensure and certifications generally require some level of continued education to keep them active. Premium audit managers can enroll in relevant coursework offered at several colleges and universities. Additionally, credit could be awarded for participation in conferences, seminars, and workshops in various areas related to the field, such as insurance, auditing, financial accounting, or risk management.

How to Prepare for a Workers Compensation Audit

Part 1. Gathering Required Records

1. Ask what you need to provide. You shouldn't volunteer more information than requested. For this reason, you should ask what documents the auditor needs to see and then gather those documents ahead of time.

2. Collect payroll records. The auditor will probably request payroll records, so get these in order. Generally, you must provide copies of the following:

- Payroll journal and summary (payroll includes salaries, wages, commissions, overtime pay, and bonuses)
- State unemployment reports

- Individual earnings records
- Federal tax reports (941 reports)
- Your check book
- All overtime payments (broken out by employee)

3. Pull together your employee records. You'll probably also need to provide detailed employee records, which you should pull together before the auditor arrives. Find the following:

- Number of employees
- Hours, days and weeks worked during the year
- Detailed explanation of job duties for every employee
- Breakdown based on dollar amounts if an employee works in more than one classification code

4. Find your cash disbursements. You'll need to present this information to the auditor, so find it ahead of time. Double check to make sure all numbers are accurate:

- Payments to any subcontractors and independent contractors
- Materials
- Casual labor

5. Gather your certificates of insurance. Depending on your state, you may be charged workers' compensation premiums for independent contractors and subcontractors. You'll want current certificates of insurance for every subcontractor you used during the policy period.

- The certificates should state that workers' compensation insurance is being provided. Some contractors have only general liability coverage without workers' compensation.
- In some states, sole proprietors and partners can opt out of the workers' compensation requirement.

Part 2. Setting up for the Audit

1. Determine your type of audit. You might have one of two kinds of audits: a physical audit or a voluntary audit. You should know ahead of time which you will have:

- A physical audit involves an auditor contacting you by phone or mail and scheduling an appointment. They must contact you within 60 days of the expiration of your policy. You will provide the auditor with documents. The auditor is working on a deadline—usually thirty days once assigned your audit.
- A voluntary audit involves you receiving a form in the mail from your insurance company. You must complete the form and submit it to your insurer. Although the forms are basic, you should call the insurer if you have any questions.

2. Identify a primary contact. The audit will go more smoothly if your business designates a primary contact to work with the insurer. Make sure to choose someone who is familiar with the entire business. This person should also be familiar with payroll records.

This primary contact should be familiar with any prior audits. They should review the auditor's worksheets and prior policies so that they are aware of the issues that can arise.

3. Clear out a space for the auditor. The auditor might work off the premises. However, if they work in your office, then make a comfortable space for them to work. It should be well-lit and quiet.

- Try to get the auditor to work on your premises. This makes sharing information easier, and you can provide as much detailed information as possible. It can be hard to share information when auditors work off-site.

4. Review the original policy. This policy was based on an estimate. However, you should review the policy to uncover what was used to calculate your initial policy premiums. Consider the following:

- Payrolls. Workers compensation rates are typically tied to your payroll. For every hundred dollars, you are charged a rate.
- Rate. The rate will be based on the kind of work done. This work will be classified based on a classification system used to determine workers' comp.
- Classification codes. Not all work carries the same likelihood of injury. The auditor will determine what is the governing classification that generates the most payroll. However, some workers are given their own classification, such as clerical and outside sales people.
- Experience modification factor. After determining the classification, the auditor multiplies the rate by your payroll. However, the auditor can adjust this amount based on your prior workers' compensation history.

5. Analyze public information about your company. Look at your website and see if there is any information there that is wrong. Your auditor will be reviewing all publicly available information about your business. You should correct anything that is inaccurate.

Part 3. Handling the Audit

1. Maintain a professional relationship with the auditor. The audit can be stressful because the insurer might drastically increase your premiums. You can make the process go more smoothly by always being friendly and helpful to the auditor.

- Based on your policy, the auditor probably can request any financial document, such as tax filings. You should provide it promptly and without disagreement.

- You would rather the auditor work with the accurate information than guess. When auditors guess, they provide "worst case scenario" information, which likely inflates your premiums.
- You can typically expect to pay 25% more when you don't comply with the auditor.

2. Review the auditor's worksheets. Sometimes auditors make mistakes that benefit the insurance company (and hurt you). You should carefully review the auditor's work after they finish. You will have to ask the insurer for copies of the auditor's worksheets.

- An insurer doesn't generally offer these worksheets unless you ask.
- Avoid signing off on any audit that is incomplete.

3. Compare the audit to the original policy. Sometimes, the audited premiums will be higher than the estimate you received when you bought the policy. You want to make sure any increase is legitimate. Look for the following:

- Whether the experience modification factor is higher on the audit than on the original policy. It shouldn't be.
- If there are more expensive classification codes on the audit than in the original policy. Sometimes, your business operations change so these classifications will change. However, they generally shouldn't absent a major change in your operations.

- Whether the schedule credit or debit has changed. If so, you might be able to dispute the amount.

4. Meet with an insurance attorney. If you have questions, then schedule a consultation with a lawyer. Show them the auditor's worksheets and your original policy. Your lawyer can decide whether you have grounds for challenging the audit.

- You can find an insurance attorney by contacting your state or local bar association and asking for a referral.
- You can find your nearest bar association by visiting the American Bar Association's website: http://shop.americanbar.org/ebus/ABAGroups/DivisionforBarServices/BarAssociationDirectories/StateLocalBarAssociations.aspx. Enter your address.
- Call up and schedule a consultation. Make sure to ask how much it will cost.

5. Dispute the audit. Your insurer should tell you how to dispute the audit determination. For example, you might need to submit records to the insurer within a certain amount of time. If you wait too long, then the insurer will probably assume you agree with the audit.

- Don't delay. Call up your insurer and complain that you don't agree with the audit. Ask what you need to provide and the deadline.

External Auditor

An external auditor performs an audit, in accordance with specific laws or rules, of the financial statements of a company, government entity, other legal entity, or organization, and is independent of the entity being audited. Users of these entities' financial information, such as investors, government agencies, and the general public, rely on the external auditor to present an unbiased and independent audit report.

The manner of appointment, the qualifications, and the format of reporting by an external auditor are defined by statute, which varies according to jurisdiction. External auditors must be members of one of the recognised professional accountancy bodies. External auditors normally address their reports to the shareholders of a corporation. In the United States, certified public accountants are the only authorized non-governmental external auditors who may perform audits and attestations on an entity's financial statements and provide reports on such audits for public review. In the UK, Canada and other Commonwealth nations Chartered Accountants and Certified General Accountants have served in that role.

For public companies listed on stock exchanges in the United States, the Sarbanes-Oxley Act (SOX) has imposed stringent requirements on external auditors in their evaluation of internal controls and financial reporting. In many countries external auditors of nationalized commercial entities are appointed by an independent government body such as the Comptroller and Auditor General. Securities and Exchange Commissions may also impose specific requirements and roles on external auditors, including strict rules to establish independence.

CHAPTER

5

Auditing Processes

This chapter explores the varied auditing processes, such as conducting an operational audit, conducting an audit program, performing an internal audit, conducting a tax audit, developing an effective compliance audit process, etc. These topics will enable an easy understanding of the processes involved in auditing.

How to Conduct an Operational Audit

There are typically six steps in an operational audit that range from preparatory work conducting interviews and collecting documents to the presentation of the final written report. An audit should be customized to meet a company's specific needs, so standard steps can only serve as a guideline. Management and its internal and external auditors will adjust the process to address the company's particular goals and objectives.

An operational audit is a review of the internal processes of a company. Its goals are to determine if company resources are being used efficiently and to identify ways to improve systems. The review includes various tasks, such as financial controls, the condition of equipment, and human resources allocations. Larger companies typically have an internal audit department that will handle the operational audit. Some companies will bring in outside consultants who specialize in operational reviews to do the audit or to work in conjunction with internal staff.

The first step in an operational audit is to structure the upcoming review. This could entail holding a meeting to outline expectations and to answer questions about the process. An external auditor will use this step to gather pertinent information about the company and set goals and objectives for the audit. This introductory step establishes the scope of the review.

Steps two and three of the audit are the surveys of management and of the employees. Managers are typically interviewed for details concerning company systems and procedures. Employees are interviewed and observed in their work environments. Observation can lead to important insights into operational deficiencies that would not be evident through an interview.

The presentation of the audit plan is typically the fourth step in an operational audit. An audit plan is a written agenda that details the steps the company will have to follow to complete the audit. It is customized and based on the information the auditor gathered in the previous steps.

Step five is the actual audit. The auditor implements the audit plan, which ordinarily includes a review of the company's productivity and sales efforts. On the financial side, he assesses billing, cash flow management, and reporting processes. The company's risk management procedures are also ordinarily included in the audit. An operational audit can include these areas and any others that management thinks need a third party assessment.

In the sixth step, the auditor produces a final written report. It details his conclusions and recommendations. This report can be hundreds of pages long, depending upon the size of the company and the number of operational areas that were included in the audit.

How to Conduct a Successful Audit Program

1. Track risk assessments annually and centrally. By tracking audit risk assessments and data in one place, it allows to start comparing risk over time and build trending reports on risk. This can be value in the annual audit report to executive management.

2. Review management requests and items for audit plans. Document any management requests and review prior to the develop of the annual audit plan. Make sure to think about any meetings and team projects, association group participation, training and development, research and development, assistance with examiners and auditors, and other administrative tasks.

3. Manage internal and external findings with a notification tool. Track status, assigned to, due date, follow ups for all internal and external items to resolve in timely manner. Create notifications to department managers to assign and resolve findings.

4. Determine level of management response needed and requirements. Define core management team that will be responsible for responding and mitigating findings based on requirements. Create expectations of what is to be completed and the depth of the response that is needed.

5. Define methodology of risk assessments and audit process and add to audit plan. Make sure the audit process and methodology is well documented and added to the annual audit plan. This should be easy to understand and explain all critical items and processes that are completed within audit program.

6. Create oversight reports for trending and gap analysis. It can make it easier to review and analyze data for the year when it is summarized in pie charts or other visuals.

7. Mitigate and manage external findings through action items. Create reportable action items that can be assigned to management. From there, you can base notifications on due dates and hold management accountable for responses.

8. Develop audit testing that is repeatable and has controls. Define audit tests and schedules based on a repeatable process. Then create reports and oversight charts to manage the process and make sure the testing is accurate.

9. Use a few departments as initial launch for user level training for any software program. Once admins have been trained and data is in the software, create a few pilot department managers to help with any new process. Once confirmed there are no issues, then release to the entire group of management.

10. Determine realistic deadlines and timelines. Map out tasks, capacity and time to ensure that any due dates and the overall audit timeline is reasonable for the organization.

How to Perform an Internal Audit

1. Identify Areas that Need Auditing

Internal audits are one tool that organizations use to ensure that their products and services are delivered the right way, the first time and every time. Identify departments that operate by using policies and procedures written by the organization or by regulatory agencies. This can include areas as complex as manufacturing processes or as simplistic as accounting procedures. Make a list of each area and the functions of the area that require review.

2. Determine How Often Auditing Needs to be Done

Some areas may only need to be audited annually while some departments may require more frequent audits. For example, a manufacturing process may require daily audits for quality control purposes while the HR function may only require an annual audit of records and processes.

3. Create Audit Calendar

A structured and systematic approach to the auditing process can help ensure the function gets completed. And, like any other business goal, audits should be integrated into corporate objectives. Scheduling audits on the business calendar ensures that it is done consistently.

4. Alert Departments of Scheduled Audits

It is simply common courtesy to give departments notice of an audit so they can have the necessary documents and materials ready and available for the reviewer. A surprise audit should only be done if there is suspicion of unethical or illegal activity. Department managers should not feel threatened by an auditor but view them as a valued resource to help them better manage their area.

5. Be Prepared

The auditor should come prepared with an understanding of policies and procedures and a list of items that will be reviewed. For example, an HR audit may focus on employee files and I-9 compliance. The more prepared the auditor is the more efficient the process will be and the less down time there will be for the area being reviewed.

6. Interview Users

The auditor should interview employees and ask them to explain their work process. Compare the process, as the employee explained it, to what the written policy says. This step is to gain an understanding of employee competence and identify areas that need additional training.

7. Document Results

Document the results and any differences in practice to how the policies are written, when policies are complied with and when they are not. This may also include other information that is gathered from the interview process. Again, the goal is to identify gaps in compliance and to figure out a way to bridge that gap.

8. Report Findings

Create an easy to read audit report. These reports should be reviewed with senior management and an improvement plan should be developed for areas that have gaps in practice compliance. Using a FOCUS PDCA model can help facilitate a structured process for implementing this type of improvement.

Other things to think about

- When reviewing policies and procedures, it is important to think about whether they are meeting the needs of customers and adding value to the organization.
- Policies and procedures should focus on continuous improvement as it relates to how work is performed.

- Is there a strong team environment that supports compliance with policies and procedures? A dysfunctional team can impact procedural compliance.
- Policies and procedures should be reviewed on an annual basis to ensure policies reflect the changing business environment.

How to Conduct a Quality Audit

Quality audits are an important part of helping small businesses grow and prosper because they provide a way to assess the business's efficiency and cost-management strategies. Whether the audit focuses on products or processes, the results helps managers determine how well strategies are working, identify the underlying cause of problems and, if necessary, take corrective action. Knowing how to conduct an internal quality audit is an important step in ensuring the success of your business.

Preliminary Review

The steps you take before conducting an on-site quality review can determine the audit's effectiveness. The process starts by formulating a detailed audit plan that functions as a road map for conducting an on-site review. Specify the timeline, scope of the audit and audit location. Collect and review written documentation, including the quality management policy for the product or process, standard operating procedures and manuals. Decide on and develop a preliminary list of personal interviews to conduct during the on-site review. Keep in mind that a preliminary list, which typically includes the department manager or supervisor and key employees, may expand during the active audit phase.

Assemble Audit Documents

Each audit team member should have an audit checklist as well as forms, or a tape recorder, for recording information during personal interviews. Each member should also have reference documents such as copies of standard operating procedures. A checklist is critical for recording information and observations, as well as for making sure you don't forget anything. While specific checklist items will vary depending on the department, product or process being audited, the checklist typically consists of sections, evaluation items within each section, a rating system and a space for comments. Common sections include department organization, the physical work environment, quality system components such as SOPs, and performance testing.

Conducting the On-site Audit

The on-site review focuses on gathering the information you'll need to determine whether the department in question is adhering to quality control standards and following established quality control procedures. This phase consists of action steps, including observation, testing and conducting personal interviews. Most often, the audit team completes certain tasks, such as performance or quality testing and personal interviews, behind the scenes. This helps the team avoid interrupting daily operations as much as possible. It's important to understand that just as with personal interviews, both an audit plan and checklist may expand in scope and depth of evaluation, depending on what you discover during the active audit phase.

Finish and Follow-Up Activities

The "real" work starts once the active phase of the audit is complete. The final phase of a quality audit starts with a meeting to review, address and determine the steps needed to correct quality issues and problematic areas. Create a management report detailing this information. Once the owner and managers finish reviewing the audit findings, a strategy meeting should be held that focuses on analyzing and deciding how -- and sometimes whether -- to incorporate solutions for quality improvements presented by the audit team.

How to Develop an Effective Compliance Audit Process

An effective compliance audit process ensures your company is following regulations and avoiding sanctions. This is especially important in public companies, as these entities are subject to federal examination. By developing and enacting an effective compliance audit process, the company accomplishes two things. First, it gives itself the best chance to catch compliance issues before they become a problem. Second, it shows the federal examiners that the company is doing everything in its power to adhere to the required regulations.

1. Select a team to perform the audit. For maximum effectiveness, select experienced and highly detail-oriented individuals. Appoint the most qualified candidate to oversee the team.
2. Segregate different areas of the company to audit. Prioritize the order in which each department will be examined. Start with high-risk areas that are subject to greater regulatory scrutiny, such as accounting or processing.
3. Obtain copies of departmental procedures for each area you intend to audit. Cross-reference the procedures against regulations to make sure none are in apparent violation.
4. Review all reports pertaining to production and volume. Use this to determine the sample size to audit. Examining 100 out of 500 loans is a good sample size. Examining 100 out of 10,000 loans will not provide enough information. Adjust the size of your audit team accordingly.
5. Determine a timeline. Since audits are often disruptive to daily functions, care should be taken to allow the departments to maintain daily routines as much as possible, while still allotting time to complete the review thoroughly.
6. Create a checklist of items each auditor should observe when reviewing a file. For example, when reviewing a commercial loan file, the auditor should review the underwriting, commitment letter, loan documents, appraisals, environmental studies and supporting documentation.

7. Develop a system for reporting your findings and recommendations. Ensure that all information is arranged in a logical and easily understood manner.

How to Conduct Tax Audit

Step 1: Get all the books of accounts of your client for the previous year whose audit is being conducted.

Step 2: Read the form 3CD & try to keep in mind or make a separate checklist of the details which are required to completely fill up the form 3CD. Some of this information can be about – the details of fixed asset, details of inventory, previous report data, payments made to related persons, payments exceeding Rs. 20,000/- made during this previous year, etc. Also, Don't forget to take the details about TDS deducted by the assessee and also the details of Indirect Taxes paid by the assessee.

Step 3: Check the opening balances from the previous report. This is an important step & if any of the opening balances do no tally with the previous year's report, we will face difficulty in making the Balance Sheet of the current year.

Step 4: Vouching

- This is one of the most important steps in doing a Tax Audit. Vouching involves the complete checking of all the vouchers of the enterprise. Detecting the possibility of any misrepresentation or fraud done by the client is very probable at this step. Utmost care should be taken & all the vouchers should be thoroughly checked. Commonly we do cash expenses vouching, bank expenses vouching, purchase vouching, sales vouching, etc.

Step 5: Bank Reconciliation. In order to verify whether all the transactions related to bank have been duly accounted, we verify the bank book with the bank statements. If there is a mismatch of some transactions, we prepare a BRS i.e., a Bank Reconciliation Statement.

Step 6: Check whether payments exceeding Rs. 20,000/- in cash have been made? If the same are done, they need to be reported in our report. Also, we should make sure that cash is not going negative in the books of accounts in any part of the year.

Step 7: Prepare the Balance Sheet & the Profit & Loss Account. As we have to upload the scanned copies of the financial statements with our Tax audit report, make sure we make CA certified Financial Statements first & get scanned copies of the same ready.

Step 8: Ledger Scrutiny. Make sure all the ledgers of your client have been carefully overlooked by you. The general nature of the ledger & the transactions present in the ledger do not show anything unusual or exceptional. In case, it does, make sure you receive satisfactory explanation of the same from your client. Otherwise, the auditor should appropriately classify his report.

Step 9: Proper Notes & Disclosures. If you find anything worth mentioning in Step 8 or non – compliance of any of the Accounting Standards, the same should be properly reported by you, the auditor.

How to Conduct a Financial Audit

Financial audits dig deep into a company's financial situation, probing accounting records, internal controls policies, cash holdings and other sensitive financial areas. Publicly-traded corporations are subject to external financial audits on a regular basis, and even privately owned small businesses can be subjected to an external financial audit by the IRS or other government authority. Knowing how to perform a financial audit on your own books can help you to prepare for a possible external audit, keep your accounting system in order and discourage internal fraud and theft.

Gather Financial Documents

Review the systems put in place to transmit financial information to the accounting department. The first step in the accounting cycle is to gather financial documentation, such as sales receipts, invoices and bank statements, and forward it to the accounting department for processing. Without timely and reliable information, accounting records can become unreliable themselves, creating discrepancies in a company's financial records.

Look at Record-Keeping

Look into the company's record-keeping policies and check to ensure records are being stored properly. Small businesses should keep at least an electronic photocopy of cash register tapes, cancelled checks, invoices and other financial documentation until the end of the current accounting period. Make sure that archived records can be accessed quickly to shed light on any potential issues that arise.

Review the Accounting System

Identify and review each element of the company's accounting system, including individual T-accounts (debits and credits), journal entries, the general ledger and current financial statements. Systematically work through the accounting system to ensure that all necessary accounts are present, that T-accounts are posted to the general ledger in a timely manner and that the system has the ability to correct human errors, such as arithmetic mistakes.

Review the Internal Control Policies

Check into the company's internal controls policies to gauge the level of protection they provide from theft and fraud. Internal control policies include things like separation of accounting duties between different employees, locked safes for holding pending bank deposits and password-protected accounting software that tracks exactly who does what and when.

Compare Internal and External Records

Compare internal records of cash holdings, income and expenses against external records. Check the company's stored external records and compare selected transactions against internal records. Compare purchase receipts sent from suppliers for a certain month against internal purchase records, for example, or compare cash register tapes against revenue recorded on the books.

Look at Tax Records

Analyze the company's internal tax records and official tax returns. Tax records should be kept for seven years to be on the safe side. Browse through the company's tax receipts from the IRS and compare it against records of tax liabilities and taxes paid in the company's accounting records. Take a little extra time to review the range of credits and deductions claimed on the most recent tax return, looking for areas of dubious reporting, such as inflated expense numbers.

How to Conduct Investigative Audit

Step One Begin the case (Respond to Complaint, etc.)

If the case starts with a complaint or report, fully debrief the complainant, getting as much detail as possible. If the case starts with the discovery of a red flag, match the red flag to the potential scheme and then look for other red flags of the suspected schemes. An automated, "proactive" search for fraud indicators might be effective if the necessary data is available.

Step Two Evaluate the Allegations or Suspicions

Determine whether the allegations or suspicions – the "red flags" – are specific and serious enough to justify an investigation, which can be time consuming, disruptive and costly.

If you determine that a complaint or report warrants further investigation, try to make a quick, preliminary assessment of the accuracy of the complaint. For example, if the complainant alleges that he or she was unfairly disqualified from a tender, examine the relevant project files to attempt to determine if this may have occurred. Use this information to prepare for the follow up interview of the complainant.

Step Three Conduct due diligence background checks

Check on-line and other records on the suspect firms and individuals to evaluate the allegations and to look for other evidence of fraud or corruption, such as the presence of shell companies as subcontractors, prior debarments of a contractor or evidence that a project official is living beyond his means.

Step Four Complete the Internal stage of the Investigation

Complete the collection of documents, data and interviews within the investigating organization, e.g.,

- Look in the bidding documents for evidence of corrupt influence through the manipulation of the "SPQQD" factors – Selection, Pricing, Quantity, Quality and Delivery;

- Carefully examine bids and proposals, CVs and other documents submitted by a suspect firm for possible fraudulent representations;
- Access, with the proper authority, the relevant e-mail and computer hard drive information;
- Determine if an early interview of the subject is warranted.

Step Five Check for Predication and get Organized

Review the results of the investigation to date to determine if there is adequate "predication" – a sufficient factual basis – to proceed. Decide or refine your initial "Case Theory" and organize the evidence according to the elements of proof of the potential claims. If law enforcement assistance is needed (e.g., to subpoena documents, exercise search warrants or to request international legal assistance) take steps to ensure that there is sufficient "probable cause" to obtain such cooperation.

Step Six Begin the External Investigation

Conduct interviews of witnesses outside the investigating organization, proceeding from the disinterested, cooperative witnesses to "facilitators" to co-conspirators to the subjects. Request or compel documents from third parties and the suspect contractors through negotiated agreements, the exercise of contract audit rights or, if available with law enforcement assistance, subpoenas or search warrants.

Step Seven Prove Illicit Payments

Determine the best strategy to prove illicit payments: out from the point of payment (by examining the contractor's records), or back from the point of receipt (from the suspect employee's records) and begin the tracing process. If it is not possible to prove the corrupt payments directly, try to prove them circumstantially by showing the subject displayed unexplained sudden wealth or expenditures.

Step Eight Obtain the Cooperation of an Inside Witness

This could be an honest inside observer or a lesser participant in the offense, such as a middleman or the smaller of several bribe payers. Decide the best strategy to obtain his or her cooperation.

Step Nine Interview the Primary Subject

In a corruption case, conduct a thorough interview of the primary subject, usually the suspected bribe recipient. Ask about his role in the suspect contract award and relevant financial issues, such as his sources of income and expenditures. Decide if there is sufficient evidence to obtain a confession; if not, try to get helpful admissions and identify possible defenses (different objectives require different tactics.) Record the interview, if possible, and request all relevant financial and other records. In a fraud case, interview the person most knowledgeable and responsible for the suspected false statement or fraudulent document. Again, decide if there is sufficient evidence to obtain a confession and, if not, try to get helpful admissions and identify possible defenses. These typically include that any false statement was an honest mistake, or that another person was responsible for a fraudulent document. Record the interview if possible.

Step Ten Prepare the Final Report

Decide what action to recommend based on the results of the investigation – an administrative sanction or criminal referral, for example – and prepare a concise final report, organized according to the elements of proof for the relevant offenses.

Contents of Investigations Report

The investigator may draft the investigation report. The report may contain:

1. The purpose and scope of Investigation.

2. The period covered by the investigation.

3. The terms of investigation with reference to the written instructions of the client.

4. The various limitations faced by the investigator that may materially affect the conclusion drawn should be mentioned.

5. The assumption forms the basis of investigation. The assumption should not defeat the very purpose of the investigation.

6. The investigation report should contain headings, with subheadings, charts, graphs, etc.

7. Conclusion of the investigator should be stated is clear and certain terms.

8. The supporting documents and data may be presented as appendices to report.

Permissions

All chapters in this book are published with permission under the Creative Commons Attribution Share Alike License or equivalent. Every chapter published in this book has been scrutinized by our experts. Their significance has been extensively debated. The topics covered herein carry significant information for a comprehensive understanding. They may even be implemented as practical applications or may be referred to as a beginning point for further studies.

We would like to thank the editorial team for lending their expertise to make the book truly unique. They have played a crucial role in the development of this book. Without their invaluable contributions this book wouldn't have been possible. They have made vital efforts to compile up to date information on the varied aspects of this subject to make this book a valuable addition to the collection of many professionals and students.

This book was conceptualized with the vision of imparting up-to-date and integrated information in this field. To ensure the same, a matchless editorial board was set up. Every individual on the board went through rigorous rounds of assessment to prove their worth. After which they invested a large part of their time researching and compiling the most relevant data for our readers.

The editorial board has been involved in producing this book since its inception. They have spent rigorous hours researching and exploring the diverse topics which have resulted in the successful publishing of this book. They have passed on their knowledge of decades through this book. To expedite this challenging task, the publisher supported the team at every step. A small team of assistant editors was also appointed to further simplify the editing procedure and attain best results for the readers.

Apart from the editorial board, the designing team has also invested a significant amount of their time in understanding the subject and creating the most relevant covers. They scrutinized every image to scout for the most suitable representation of the subject and create an appropriate cover for the book.

The publishing team has been an ardent support to the editorial, designing and production team. Their endless efforts to recruit the best for this project, has resulted in the accomplishment of this book. They are a veteran in the field of academics and their pool of knowledge is as vast as their experience in printing. Their expertise and guidance has proved useful at every step. Their uncompromising quality standards have made this book an exceptional effort. Their encouragement from time to time has been an inspiration for everyone.

The publisher and the editorial board hope that this book will prove to be a valuable piece of knowledge for students, practitioners and scholars across the globe.

Index

A

Accountant, 2, 9, 16, 23, 56, 66, 117-118, 120, 133, 135, 137, 169

Accounting, 1-2, 7, 9-16, 24-26, 28-29, 35-37, 45-48, 50, 52-53, 60-64, 66, 69, 71, 76, 79, 97-99, 101-102, 108-110, 113-114, 124, 131-141, 156-158, 169-170, 180, 183-186

Accounting Audit, 113, 132-135, 137

Accounts Payable, 2, 15-17, 19-20, 25, 37-39, 43, 45, 53-54, 61, 77, 82, 88, 129, 134

Accounts Receivable, 2, 14-15, 18-20, 25, 37, 39-41, 43, 46, 62, 70, 76, 81, 86, 129

Accrual Accounting, 12, 47, 60, 109

Amortization, 67, 69, 95

Asset, 22, 49, 53, 61, 69, 73, 80-81, 84-88, 90, 95, 105, 118, 184

Audit Report, 6, 113-114, 139, 149-152, 154-155, 177, 179, 181, 184

Audit Trail, 134, 136

Auditor, 5-6, 113, 116-118, 120, 122-124, 126-127, 129-131, 139, 141, 144, 146-147, 151, 155-179, 181, 183-184

B

Balance Sheet, 22, 35, 45, 49-50, 54-55, 60-61, 63-67, 71-84, 87-91, 105, 107-108, 114, 184

Bank Reconciliation, 25, 184

Bill, 20, 74, 165

Bond, 126

Bookkeeper, 2-3, 6-7, 9-11, 14, 18, 24-26, 28, 35, 99, 137

Budget, 10, 71, 75, 124, 128, 131, 150

C

Cash Book, 108-109, 111

Cash Disbursements, 2, 107-108, 171

Cash Flow Statement, 107-108

Cash Receipts, 9, 107-108, 128

Chart of Accounts, 10, 37, 41, 44, 55-56, 59

Compliance Audit, 149-150, 178, 183

Credit, 2, 14-16, 21, 35-36, 38-39, 41-43 45, 51-55, 60-62, 64, 74, 79, 85, 87-88, 108-112, 137, 143, 157, 170, 176

D

Debit, 36, 38-39, 41-43, 45, 51-55, 60-62, 108-112, 137, 143, 176

Debt, 9, 38, 45, 64-65, 72, 74, 77-78, 87-91, 163-164

Depreciation, 62, 67, 69, 77, 81, 95, 106

Double-Entry Bookkeeping, 2-3, 13, 52, 60-61, 109

E

Equipment, 9, 37-39, 70, 76, 81, 84-85, 89, 138, 178

Equity, 15, 50, 53, 55, 60-61, 63-66, 71, 75-80, 83-84, 89-90, 105-108

External Audit, 5, 185

F

Finance, 4, 6, 71, 113-114, 116-118, 124, 139-141

Financial Audit, 132-133, 149-150, 185

G

General Ledger, 35, 41, 44, 46-51, 54-55, 62, 76, 79, 82, 128-130, 134, 137, 185

Gross Profit, 66-68, 93-95

I

Income Statement, 35, 49-50, 63, 66-69, 83, 87, 91-94, 105-106, 108-109, 114

Income Tax, 89, 106

Internal Accounting Audit, 132, 137

Internal Audit, 5, 115, 136, 178, 180

Internal Auditor, 118, 122, 139, 141, 144, 147, 169

Inventory, 2, 14-16, 47, 49, 52, 54-55, 61, 68, 70, 76, 78, 81, 85, 91, 93-94, 101, 104-105, 110, 114-115, 130, 137-138, 167-168, 184

Invoices, 3, 9, 19-20, 36, 39, 46, 52, 62, 110, 128, 135, 185

L

Ledger Account, 46

Loan Payments, 39, 71, 77

N

Non-Operating Income, 49, 93, 96-97, 100, 104

O

Operating Income, 49, 67-68, 92-97, 100, 103-104

Operational Audit, 149, 178-179

P

Payroll Service, 9, 25

Premium Audit Manager, 169

Profit and Loss Statement, 35, 98-105, 108-109

Q

Quickbooks, 3, 11, 35

R

Revenue, 1-2, 12-13, 15, 37, 48-49, 66, 77, 83, 93-94, 96-99, 103-104, 106, 114-115, 129, 136, 186

S

Sales, 2-3, 9, 15-16, 29, 37, 40-41, 49, 52, 62, 66-68, 70, 72, 91, 93-94, 96, 99, 103, 106, 108-112, 130, 167-169, 174, 179, 184-185

Shareholder, 4, 50, 63-66, 122

Single-Entry Bookkeeping, 2, 13, 108, 110

T

Tax Audit, 178, 184

Tax Receipts, 138, 186

Tax Return, 38, 90, 186

Total Liability, 87, 89, 91

Trial Balance, 46, 51-52, 57, 62-63, 112, 137

V

Vouching, 184

Printed in the USA
CPSIA information can be obtained
at www.ICGtesting.com
LVHW082343201023
761596LV00010B/1700